Jon + Grace —   Dec. 2001
Have fun!   Mike & Sherry

D0598049

Jon + Grace —   Dec. 2001
Have fun!   Mike & Sherry

THE ESSENTIAL
THAI
COOKBOOK

THE ESSENTIAL
THAI
COOKBOOK

LEARN THE SECRETS OF AN
EXOTIC CUISINE

Kit Chan

HERMES
HOUSE

First published in 1998 by Hermes House

© Anness Publishing Limited 1998

Hermes House is an imprint of Anness Publishing Limited,
Hermes House, 88–89 Blackfriars Road, London SE1 8HA

All rights reserved. No part of this publication may be reproduced, stored in a retrieval system,
or transmitted in any way or by any means, electronic, mechanical, photocopying, recording
or otherwise, without the prior written permission of the copyright holder.

A CIP catalogue record for this book is available from the British Library

Publisher: Joanna Lorenz
Senior Cookery Editor: Linda Fraser
Cookery Editor: Maggie Mayhew
Designer: Alan Marshall, Siân Keogh
Photography and styling: Thomas Odulate
Illustrator: Madeleine David

Front Cover: Lisa Tai, Designer; Thomas Odulate, Photographer; Helen Trent, Stylist;
Marie-Ange Lapierre, Home Economist

Previously published in the Creative Cookery Library series as *Taste of Thailand*

Printed in Hong Kong/China

1 3 5 7 9 10 8 6 4 2

NOTES
For all recipes, quantities are given in both metric and imperial measures and, where
appropriate, measures are given in standard cups and spoons. Follow one set, but not a
mixture, because they are not interchangeable.

Standard spoon and cup measurements are level.
1 tsp = 5ml; 1 tbsp = 15ml; 1 cup = 250ml/8fl oz

Australian standard tablespoons are 20ml. Australian readers should use 3 tsp in place of
1 tbsp for measuring small quantities of gelatine, cornflour, salt etc.

Medium eggs should be used unless otherwise stated.

CONTENTS

INTRODUCTION

Thailand is probably one of the most diverse and complex countries in Asia. Geographically it is halfway between India and China and so it is hardly surprising that the cultures of its neighbours have influenced the development of its national cuisine.

Thailand is divided into five regions that have distinct geographical and cultural differences; from dense jungles and mountainous retreats to vast plains of paddy-fields, untamed rivers to brilliant white sandy beaches and the warm clear ocean.

The climate is tropical so there is an abundance of fruit, vegetables and flowers. The carving of fruits and vegetables into exotic sculptures, decorated with flowers and foliage, has become an art form in Thailand. It also boasts over one thousand varieties of orchids and the orchid has become an emblem for the country.

The cooking is a source of pride and wonder. A Thai cook will always strive for a balance of flavour, texture and colour in a dish. Presentation varies from simple plastic bowls at pavement stalls to beautifully decorated china and artistic displays in the finer restaurants, but the complexity of taste and flavour in their culinary magic is consistent.

The most prevalent flavour in Thai cooking comes from the chilli, which surprisingly was introduced to the country by Portuguese missionaries in the sixteenth century. It didn't take the Thais long to make good use of it, believing that chillies cool the body, stimulate the appetite and bring balance and harmony to their food.

Food is a celebration. To have to eat alone ranks high on the Thai scale of misfortunes. A Thai meal offers a combination of flavours; sweet, hot, sour, salty and sometimes bitter. Usually, in addition to the obligatory bowl of rice, there will be a variety of dishes including a soup, a curry, a steamed dish, a fried one, a salad and one or two sauces. The portion size will depend on the number of people eating. All the dishes are placed on the table at the same time and shared. They are not eaten in any particular order.

Water and tea are the most common liquid accompaniments served with a meal. Thai whisky is often drunk at festive gatherings.

Below: Thai villages nestle in the lush and beautiful countryside, where the occupants grow a wide range of fresh fruits and vegetables. These people usually sell their goods at one of the many markets.

In days gone by Thais ate with their fingers, pressing rice into small balls, which were then dipped into other dishes. Today Thais eat with a large spoon to scoop up sauces and a fork to mix and push food on to the spoon. Knives are rarely used because meat is usually served in small pieces and chopsticks are only used to eat Chinese-style noodles.

Thais tend to cook by 'feel', taking into account the tastes and preferences of their family. You should always taste and adjust the seasoning to your own taste. If you find something is too salty or too sweet and, even more importantly, if you are not used to the hotness of chillies, add a little at a time until you get a balance that you like. In short, Thai cuisine is light and fresh with delicately balanced spices and a harmony of flavours, colours and textures designed to appeal to both the eyes and the palate.

Above: Floating markets are a typical sight throughout the Thai islands, where the freshest of produce can be bought.

EQUIPMENT

You don't need specialist equipment to produce a Thai meal. In fact you will probably have most of the things already. The basic items are listed below.

A sturdy chopping board with a cleaver or a large chef's knife to use for the heavy cutting and chopping, and a small paring knife for the little jobs.

A wok is essential – for most meals this is the only type of pan you will need. Perfect for stir-frying, cooking curries and simmered dishes as well as for deep-frying and steaming.

A large steamer basket is useful. The most usual are those made of bamboo that can be purchased quite cheaply from Oriental stores.

A large granite or heavy pestle and mortar for grinding spices and pounding curry paste to give the sort of texture required for Thai food. Although a coffee grinder or blender can be used instead, do bear in mind that the pungent flavours may linger.

If you eat rice regularly, you could think about investing in an electric rice cooker. It does the job well and frees up the stove top as well as making burnt rice pans a thing of the past.

Equipment (clockwise from top): two-tier bamboo steamer, large granite pestle and mortar, wooden chopping board with cleaver, large cook's knife and small paring knife, a wire basket draining spoon and wok.

INGREDIENTS

AUBERGINES
A vegetable fruit with a mildly sweet flavour. Many varieties of aubergine are used in Thai cooking, from tiny pea aubergines, which are added just before the end of cooking, to white, yellow or green aubergines. When these types are unavailable, substitute with the purple variety.

Clockwise from top left: green aubergines, yellow aubergines, pea aubergines and purple aubergines.

BAMBOO SHOOTS
The edible young shoots of the bamboo plant. Pale to bright yellow when bought fresh. Fresh shoots need some preparation and take quite a long time to cook. When buying canned shoots, look out for the whole ones as they seem to be better quality than the ready-sliced canned bamboo shoots.

BANANA LEAVES
Glossy, dark green leaves of the banana tree are used to line steamers or to wrap foods such as chicken or fish prior to grilling or baking. They impart a vague flavour of fine tea.

BASIL
A pungent herb much used in the Mediterranean regions and in South-East Asia. Three varieties of basil are used in Thai cooking – *bai mangluk* (hairy basil), *bai horapa* (sweet basil) and *bai grapao* (Thai or Holy basil), which tastes hot and slightly medicinal. *Bai horapa* is the most popular. It has small, dark leaves with reddish-purple stems

and flowers. Its flavour is reminiscent of aniseed and somewhat stronger than that of the western sweet basil.

BEAN CURD
Most often used in soups and Chinese dishes. It is made from soy beans and is rich in vitamins and minerals. It is usually sold in square blocks packed in water. Bean curd comes in many forms – fresh, fried and dried.

BEANSPROUTS
Sprouted from mung beans, they are used in salads and stir-fried dishes. Rich in vitamins, protein and iron, beansprouts are widely available in supermarkets. Look for crisp, firm sprouts with little scent.

BEAN SAUCE
Made from salted, fermented soy beans, this sauce is a popular flavouring agent in oriental dishes. It is also called yellow bean sauce.

CHILLI
There are many different kinds of chillies. The small, red and green fresh chillies, known as Thai or bird's eye, are extremely hot. Larger varieties are slightly milder. The 'fire' comes from the seeds so discard them if a milder flavour is preferred. Chillies contain volatile oil that can irritate the skin and cause eyes to burn. Always wash your hands immediately after using them.

Clockwise from top left: Thai or Holy basil, lemon basil and hairy basil.

Left: fresh drained beancurd; right: fried bean curd cubes.

COCONUT MILK
This unsweetened liquid made from grated coconut flesh and water, is an essential ingredient of many Thai dishes. It is available in cans, compressed blocks or in powder form.

CORIANDER
The leaves and seeds of the coriander plant are one of the most essential in Thai cooking. The root is also used, often pounded with garlic and other ingredients, to make a marinade.

Clockwise from top: green chillies, Thai orange chillies, Indian chillies, red chillies, and mild green chillies.

CURRY PASTE
This is traditionally made in a mortar by pounding together fresh herbs and spices. There are several kinds. Home-made curry pastes take time and effort to prepare but they taste wonderful and keep well. Ready-made pastes, which come in packets or tubs, are a good alternative and enable cooks to make tasty curries quickly.

FISH SAUCE (NAM PLA)

The most commonly used flavouring in Thai food. Fish sauce is used in Thai cooking the same way soy sauce is used in Chinese dishes. It is made from salted anchovies and has a strong salty flavour.

GALANGAL

A member of the ginger family that looks similar to fresh root ginger, but with a more translucent skin and a pinkish tinge. It has a wonderful sharp, lemony taste and it is prepared in a similar fashion to root ginger. Best used fresh, it is also available dried or in powder form.

Clockwise from top left: pickled garlic, fresh root ginger, fresh turmeric, fresh garlic, Galangal root.

GARLIC

Garlic is indispensable in Thai cooking. Heads of the Asian variety are quite small. Look out for fresh shiny heads of garlic with no soft, dusty or mouldy cloves. Jars of pickled garlic can be bought from Oriental stores.

GINGER

A root of Chinese and Indian origin. It is always used fresh rather than dried and should be peeled and chopped or crushed before cooking. It is available in supermarkets. Look for shiny fat roots that aren't wrinkled or shrivelled. Though not used as frequently as galangal in Thai cooking, ginger makes a good alternative to galangal.

KAFFIR LIME

This is similar to the common lime but has a knobbly skin. The zest of the fruit is often used and the dark glossy green leaves from the tree impart a pungent lemony-lime flavour to soups, curries and other dishes. You can buy them fresh in Oriental stores. They keep well and can be frozen. Dried Kaffir limes are also available.

LEMON GRASS

Also known as citronella, lemon grass has long pale green stalks and a bulbous end similar to a spring onion. Only the bottom 12cm/5in is used. It has a woody texture and an aromatic lemony scent. Unless finely chopped, it is always removed before serving because it is so fibrous.

PALM SUGAR

Strongly-flavoured, hard brown sugar made from the sap of the coconut palm tree. Available in Oriental stores. If you have trouble finding it, use soft dark brown sugar instead.

ROASTED GROUND RICE

Raw glutinous rice grains are dry-fried until brown, then ground to a powder. A traditional ingredient in salads.

Clockwise from top left: water spinach, taramind pods, snake beans, garlic shoots and garlic chives.

Clockwise from top: lemon grass, Thai shallots, kaffir limes and fresh kaffir lime leaves.

SALTED EGGS

A traditional way of preserving duck eggs in Asia. You can find them in most Oriental stores, often sold covered in a thick layer of charcoal-grey ash. Rub off the ash with your finger under running water and then hard-boil the eggs.

SHALLOTS

Thai shallots have a lovely pinkish-purple colour and are used extensively in Thai cuisine instead of onions.

SOY SAUCE

Made from fermented soy beans, soy sauce is available in light or dark versions and can be quite salty. It is the background seasoning to many stir-fried and noodle dishes.

TAMARIND

An acidic tropical fruit that resembles a bean pod. It is usually sold dried or pulped. To make tamarind juice, take 25g/1oz of tamarind or about 2 stock cube-size pieces and leave to soak in 150ml/¼ pint/⅔ cup warm water for about 10 minutes. Squeeze out as much tamarind juice as possible by pressing all the liquid through a sieve and use as in the recipes.

VINEGAR

Thais use a mild, plain white vinegar. Cider or Japanese rice wine vinegar can be used instead.

SNACKS
AND
APPETIZERS

Food and snacking are inescapable parts of life in Bangkok. Indeed, throughout the whole of Thailand a constant supply of spicy titbits are available at roadside stalls and market places.

The variety of snacks is huge. Some dishes are small, such as savoury pastries, spring rolls, steamed dumplings and rice balls. Others, such as noodle dishes, are more substantial and can be a meal in themselves. These snacks are not considered real food in Asia, but merely a pleasurable diversion to while away any spare time, a nibble between meals or a treat at the market.

Starters as such are not common in a Thai meal as all the dishes are brought to the table at once. The dishes in this chapter will serve well as a snack at drinks parties or as part of a main meal, but will also make excellent starters if you wish to serve them as a separate course.

Rice Cakes with Spicy Dipping Sauce

Rice cakes are a classic Thai appetizer. They are easy to make and can be kept in an airtight box almost indefinitely.

INGREDIENTS

Serves 4–6
175g/6oz/1 cup jasmine rice
350ml/12fl oz/1½ cups water
oil for frying and greasing

For the spicy dipping sauce
6–8 dried chillies
2.5ml/½ tsp salt
2 shallots, chopped
2 garlic cloves, chopped
4 coriander roots
10 white peppercorns
250ml/8fl oz/1 cup coconut milk
5ml/1 tsp shrimp paste
115g/4oz minced pork
115g/4oz cherry tomatoes, chopped
15ml/1 tbsp fish sauce
15ml/1 tbsp palm sugar
30ml/2 tbsp tamarind juice
30 ml/2 tbsp coarsely chopped
   roasted peanuts
2 spring onions, finely chopped

1 Stem the chillies and remove most of the seeds. Soak the chillies in warm water for 20 minutes. Drain and transfer to a mortar.

2 Add the salt and grind with a pestle until the chillies are crushed. Add the shallots, garlic, coriander roots and peppercorns. Pound together until you have a coarse paste.

3 Pour the coconut milk into a saucepan and boil until it begins to separate. Add the pounded chilli paste. Cook for 2–3 minutes until it is fragrant. Stir in the shrimp paste. Cook for another minute.

4 Add the pork, stirring to break up any lumps. Cook for about 5–10 minutes. Add the tomatoes, fish sauce, palm sugar and tamarind juice. Simmer until the sauce thickens.

5 Stir in the chopped peanuts and spring onions. Remove from the heat and leave to cool.

6 Wash the rice in several changes of water. Put in a saucepan, add the water and cover with a tight-fitting lid. Bring to the boil, reduce the heat and simmer gently for about 15 minutes.

7 Remove the lid and fluff up the rice. Turn out on to a lightly greased tray and press down with the back of a large spoon. Leave to dry out overnight in a very low oven until it is completely dry and firm.

8 Remove the rice from the tray and break into bite-size pieces. Heat the oil in a wok or deep-fat fryer.

9 Deep fry the rice cakes in batches for about 1 minute, until they puff up, taking care not to brown them too much. Remove and drain. Serve accompanied with the dipping sauce.

Spring Rolls

These crunchy spring rolls are as popular in Thai cuisine as they are in the Chinese. Thais fill their version with a garlic, pork and noodle filling.

INGREDIENTS

Makes about 24

4–6 dried Chinese mushrooms, soaked
50g/2oz bean thread noodles, soaked
30ml/2 tbsp vegetable oil
2 garlic cloves, chopped
2 red chillies, seeded and chopped
225g/8oz minced pork
50g/2oz chopped cooked prawns
30ml/2 tbsp fish sauce
5ml/1 tsp granulated sugar
1 carrot, finely shredded
50g/2oz bamboo shoots, chopped
50g/2oz beansprouts
2 spring onions, chopped
15ml/1 tbsp chopped coriander
30ml/2 tbsp flour
24 x 15cm/6in square spring roll wrappers
freshly ground black pepper
oil for frying

1 Drain and chop the mushrooms. Drain the noodles and cut into short lengths, about 5cm/2in.

2 Heat the oil in a wok or frying pan, add the garlic and chillies and fry for 30 seconds. Add the pork, stirring until the meat is browned.

3 Add the noodles, mushrooms and prawns. Season with fish sauce, sugar and pepper. Tip into a bowl.

4 Mix in the carrot, bamboo shoots, beansprouts, spring onions and chopped coriander for the filling.

5 Put the flour in a small bowl and mix with a little water to make a paste. Place a spoonful of filling in the centre of a spring roll wrapper.

6 Turn the bottom edge over to cover the filling, then fold in the left and right sides. Roll the wrapper up almost to the top edge. Brush the top edge with flour paste and seal. Repeat with the rest of the wrappers.

7 Heat the oil in a wok or deep-fat fryer. Slide in the spring rolls a few at a time and fry until crisp and golden brown. Remove with a slotted spoon and drain on kitchen paper. Serve hot with Thai sweet chilli sauce to dip them into, if liked.

Pork Satay

Originating in Indonesia, satay are skewers of meat marinated with spices and grilled quickly over charcoal. It's street food at its best, prepared by vendors with portable grills who set up stalls at every street corner and market place. You can make satay with chicken, beef or lamb. Serve with Satay Sauce and Cucumber Relish.

INGREDIENTS

Makes about 20
450g/1lb lean pork
5ml/1 tsp grated root ginger
1 stalk lemon grass, finely chopped
3 garlic cloves, finely chopped
15ml/1 tbsp medium curry paste
5ml/1 tsp ground cumin
5ml/1 tsp ground turmeric
60ml/4 tbsp coconut cream
30ml/2 tbsp fish sauce
5ml/1 tsp granulated sugar
20 wooden satay skewers
oil for cooking

For the satay sauce
250 ml/8fl oz/1 cup coconut milk
30ml/2 tbsp red curry paste
75g/3oz crunchy peanut butter
120ml/4fl oz/½ cup chicken stock
45ml/3 tbsp brown sugar
30ml/2 tbsp tamarind juice
15ml/1 tbsp fish sauce
2.5ml/1 tsp salt

1 Cut the pork thinly into 5cm/2in strips. Mix together the ginger, lemon grass, garlic, medium curry paste, cumin, turmeric, coconut cream, fish sauce and sugar.

2 Pour over the pork and leave to marinate for about 2 hours.

3 Meanwhile, make the sauce. Heat the coconut milk over a medium heat, then add the red curry paste, peanut butter, chicken stock and sugar.

4 Cook and stir until smooth, about 5–6 minutes. Add the tamarind juice, fish sauce and salt to taste.

5 Thread the meat on to skewers. Brush with oil and grill over charcoal or under a preheated grill for 3–4 minutes on each side, turning occasionally, until cooked and golden brown. Serve with the satay sauce.

Lacy Duck Egg Nets

These parcels are very attractive. Thais have a special dispenser for making the nets. It is cone-shaped with holes at the bottom, to allow the egg mixture to dribble out in threads. You can use a small-hole funnel, a piping bag with a small nozzle or a squeezy bottle.

INGREDIENTS

Makes about 12–15
Filling
4 coriander roots
2 garlic cloves
10 white peppercorns
pinch of salt
45ml/3 tbsp oil
1 small onion, finely chopped
115g/4oz lean minced pork
75g/3oz shelled prawns, chopped
50g/2oz roasted peanuts, ground
5ml/1 tsp palm sugar
fish sauce, to taste

For the egg nets
6 duck eggs
coriander leaves, to serve, plus extra
  to garnish
spring onion tassels, to garnish
sliced red chillies, to garnish

1 Using a pestle and mortar, grind the coriander roots, garlic, white peppercorns and salt into a paste.

2 Heat 30ml/2 tbsp of the oil, add the paste and fry until fragrant. Add the onion and cook until softened. Add the pork and prawns and continue to stir-fry until the meat is cooked.

3 Add the peanuts, palm sugar, salt and fish sauce, to taste. Stir the mixture and continue to cook until it becomes a little sticky. Remove from the heat. Transfer the mixture into a bowl and set aside.

4 Beat the duck eggs in a bowl. Grease a non-stick frying pan with the remaining oil and heat. Using a special dispenser or one of the alternatives, trail the eggs across the pan to make a net pattern, about 13cm/5in in diameter.

5 When the net is set, carefully remove it from the pan, and repeat until all the eggs have been used up.

6 To assemble, lay a net on a board, lay a few coriander leaves on it and top with a spoonful of the filling. Turn in the edges to make a neat square shape. Repeat with the rest of the nets. Arrange on a serving dish, garnish with spring onion tassels, coriander leaves and chillies.

Son-in-law Eggs

This fascinating name comes from a story about a prospective bridegroom who wanted to impress his future mother-in-law and devised a recipe from the only other dish he knew how to make – boiled eggs. The hard-boiled eggs are deep fried and then drenched with a sweet piquant tamarind sauce.

INGREDIENTS

Serves 4–6
75g/3oz palm sugar
75ml/5 tbsp fish sauce
90ml/6 tbsp tamarind juice
oil for frying
6 shallots, finely sliced
6 garlic cloves, finely sliced
6 red chillies, sliced
6 hard-boiled eggs, shelled
lettuce, to serve
sprigs of coriander, to garnish

1 Combine the palm sugar, fish sauce and tamarind juice in a small saucepan. Bring to the boil, stirring until the sugar dissolves, then simmer for about 5 minutes.

2 Taste and add more palm sugar, fish sauce or taramind juice, if necessary. It should be sweet, salty and slightly sour. Transfer the sauce to a bowl and set aside.

3 Heat the oil in a wok or deep-fat fryer. Meanwhile, heat a couple of spoonfuls of the oil in a frying pan and fry the shallots, garlic and chillies until golden brown. Transfer the mixture to a bowl and set aside.

4 Deep-fry the eggs in the hot oil for 3–5 minutes until golden brown. Remove and drain on kitchen paper. Cut the eggs in quarters and arrange on a bed of lettuce. Drizzle with the sauce and scatter over the shallots. Garnish with sprigs of coriander.

Fried Clams with Chilli and Yellow Bean Sauce

Seafood is abundant in Thailand, especially at all of the beach holiday resorts. This delicous dish, which is simple to prepare, is one of the favourites.

INGREDIENTS

Serves 4–6
1kg/2¼lb fresh clams
30ml/2 tbsp vegetable oil
4 garlic cloves, finely chopped
15ml/1 tbsp grated root ginger
4 shallots, finely chopped
30ml/2 tbsp yellow bean sauce
6 red chillies, seeded and chopped
15ml/1 tbsp fish sauce
pinch of granulated sugar
handful of basil leaves, plus extra
  to garnish

1 Wash and scrub the clams. Heat the oil in a wok or large frying pan. Add the garlic and ginger and fry for 30 seconds, add the shallots and fry for a further minute.

2 Add the clams. Using a fish slice or spatula, turn them a few times to coat with the oil. Add the yellow bean sauce and half the red chillies.

3 Continue to cook, stirring often, until all the clams open, about 5–7 minutes. You may need to add a splash of water. Adjust the seasoning with fish sauce and a little sugar.

4 Finally add the basil and transfer to individual bowls or a platter. Garnish with the remaining red chillies and basil leaves.

Pan-steamed Mussels with Thai Herbs

Another simple dish to prepare. The lemon grass adds a refreshing tang to the mussels.

INGREDIENTS

Serves 4–6
1kg/2¼lb mussels, cleaned and
  beards removed
2 stalks lemon grass, finely chopped
4 shallots, chopped
4 kaffir lime leaves, roughly torn
2 red chillies, sliced
15ml/1 tbsp fish sauce
30ml/2 tbsp lime juice
2 spring onions, chopped, to garnish
coriander leaves, to garnish

1 Place all the ingredients, except for the spring onions and coriander, in a large saucepan and stir thoroughly.

2 Cover and steam for 5–7 minutes, shaking the saucepan occasionally, until the mussels open. Discard any mussels that do not open.

3 Transfer the cooked mussels to a serving dish.

4 Garnish the mussels with chopped spring onions and coriander leaves. Serve immediately.

Fish Cakes with Cucumber Relish

These wonderful small fish cakes are a very familiar and popular appetizer. They are usually accompanied with Thai beer.

INGREDIENTS

Makes about 12

300g/11oz white fish fillet, such as cod,
 cut into chunks
30ml/2 tbsp red curry paste
1 egg
30ml/2 tbsp fish sauce
5ml/1 tsp granulated sugar
30ml/2 tbsp cornflour
3 kaffir lime leaves, shredded
15ml/1 tbsp chopped coriander
50g/2oz green beans, finely sliced
oil for frying
Chinese mustard cress, to garnish

For the cucumber relish

60ml/4 tbsp Thai coconut or
 rice vinegar
60ml/4 tbsp water
50g/2oz sugar
1 head pickled garlic
1 cucumber, quartered and sliced
4 shallots, finely sliced
15ml/1 tbsp finely chopped root ginger

1 To make the cucumber relish, bring the vinegar, water and sugar to the boil. Stir until the sugar dissolves, then remove from the heat and cool.

2 Combine the rest of the relish ingredients together in a bowl and pour over the vinegar mixture.

3 Combine the fish, curry paste and egg in a food processor and process well. Transfer the mixture to a bowl, add the rest of the ingredients, except for the oil and garnish, and mix well.

4 Mould and shape the mixture into cakes about 5cm/2in in diameter and 5mm/¼in thick.

5 Heat the oil in a wok or deep-fat fryer. Fry the fish cakes, a few at a time, for about 4–5 minutes or until golden brown. Remove and drain on kitchen paper. Garnish with Chinese mustard cress and serve with the cucumber relish.

Crisp-fried Crab Claws

INGREDIENTS

Serves 4
50g/2oz rice flour
15ml/1 tbsp cornflour
2.5ml/½ tsp granulated sugar
1 egg
60ml/4 tbsp cold water
1 stalk lemon grass, finely chopped
2 garlic cloves, finely chopped
15ml/1 tbsp chopped coriander
1–2 red chillies, seeded and chopped
5ml/1 tsp fish sauce
oil for frying
12 half-shelled crab claws
freshly ground black pepper

Chilli vinegar dip
45ml/3 tbsp sugar
120ml/4fl oz/½ cup water
120ml/4fl oz/½ cup red wine vinegar
15ml/1 tbsp fish sauce
2–4 red chillies, seeded and chopped

1 To make the chilli dip, put the sugar and water in a saucepan and bring to the boil, stirring until the sugar dissolves. Lower the heat and simmer for 5–7 minutes. Stir in the rest of the ingredients and set aside.

2 Combine the rice flour, cornflour and sugar in a large bowl. Beat the egg with the cold water, then stir the liquid into the flour mixture and mix well until it forms a light batter.

3 Add the lemon grass, garlic, coriander, red chillies, fish sauce and freshly ground black pepper.

4 Heat the oil in a wok or deep fat fryer. Pat dry the crab claws and dip one at a time in the batter. Gently drop the battered claws in the hot oil, a few at a time. Fry until golden brown. Drain on kitchen paper. Serve hot with the chilli vinegar dip.

Golden Pouches

These crisp pouches are delicious served as an appetizer or to accompany drinks at a party.

INGREDIENTS

Makes about 20
115g/4oz minced pork
115g/4oz crab meat
2–3 wood ears, soaked and chopped
15ml/1 tbsp chopped coriander
5ml/1 tsp chopped garlic
30ml/2 tbsp chopped spring onion
1 egg
15ml/1 tbsp fish sauce
5ml/1 tsp soy sauce
pinch of granulated sugar
freshly ground black pepper
20 wonton wrappers
20 chives, blanched (optional)
oil for deep frying
plum or sweet chilli sauce, to serve

1 In a mixing bowl, combine the pork, crab meat, wood ears, coriander, garlic, spring onions and egg. Mix well and season with fish sauce, soy sauce, sugar and freshly ground black pepper.

2 Take a wonton wrapper and place it on a flat surface. Put a heaped teaspoonful of filling in the centre of the wrapper, then pull up the edges of the pastry around the filling.

3 Pinch together to seal. If you like, you can go a step further and tie it with a long chive. Repeat with the remaining pork mixture.

4 Heat the oil in a wok or deep fat fryer. Fry the wontons in batches until they are crisp and golden brown. Drain on kitchen paper and serve immediately with either a plum or sweet chilli sauce.

Steamed Seafood Packets

Very neat and delicate, these
steamed packets make an
excellent starter or a light lunch.

INGREDIENTS
Serves 4
225g/8oz crab meat
50g/2oz shelled prawns, chopped
6 water chestnuts, chopped
30ml/2 tbsp chopped bamboo shoots
15ml/1 tbsp chopped spring onion
5ml/1 tsp chopped root ginger
15ml/1 tbsp soy sauce
15ml/1 tbsp fish sauce
12 rice sheets
banana leaves
oil for brushing
15ml/1 tbsp soy sauce
2 spring onions, shredded, to garnish
2 red chillies, seeded and sliced,
  to garnish
coriander leaves, to garnish

1 Combine the crab meat, chopped
prawns, chestnuts, bamboo shoots,
spring onion and ginger in a bowl. Mix
well, then add the soy sauce and fish
sauce. Stir until blended.

2 Take a rice sheet and dip it in
warm water. Place it on a flat surface
and leave for a few seconds to soften.

COOK'S TIP

The seafood packets will spread out when
steamed so be sure to space them well apart
to prevent them sticking together.

3 Place a spoonful of the filling in the
centre of the sheet and fold into a
square packet. Repeat with the rest of
the rice sheets and seafood mixture.

4 Use banana leaves to line a steamer,
then brush them with oil. Place the
packets, seam-side down, on the leaves
and steam over a high heat for 6–8
minutes or until the filling is cooked.
Transfer to a plate and garnish with the
remaining ingredients.

Chicken and Sticky Rice Balls

These balls can either be steamed or deep fried. The fried versions are crunchy and are excellent for serving at drinks parties.

INGREDIENTS

Makes about 30
450g/1lb minced chicken
1 egg
15ml/1 tsp tapioca flour
4 spring onions, finely chopped
30ml/2 tbsp chopped coriander
30ml/2 tbsp fish sauce
pinch of granulated sugar
freshly ground black pepper
225g/8oz cooked sticky rice
banana leaves
oil for brushing
1 small carrot, shredded, to garnish
1 red pepper, cut into strips, to garnish
snipped chives, to garnish
sweet chilli sauce, to serve

1 In a mixing bowl, combine the minced chicken, egg, tapioca flour, spring onions and coriander. Mix well and season with fish sauce, sugar and freshly ground black pepper.

2 Spread the cooked sticky rice on a plate or flat tray.

3 Place a teaspoonful of the chicken mixture on the bed of rice. With damp hands, roll and shape the mixture in the rice to make a ball about the size of a walnut. Repeat with the rest of the chicken mixture.

COOK'S TIP

Sticky rice, also known as glutinous rice, has a very high gluten content. It is so called because the grains stick together when it is cooked. It can be eaten both as a savoury and as a sweet dish.

4 Line a bamboo steamer with banana leaves and lightly brush them with oil. Place the chicken balls on the leaves, spacing well apart to prevent them sticking together. Steam over a high heat for about 10 minutes or until cooked.

5 Remove and arrange on serving plates. Garnish with shredded carrots, red pepper and chives. Serve with sweet chilli sauce to dip in.

SOUPS

Soup is a very significant part of a Thai's daily fare. It can be served as a snack or a light lunch. A bowl of soup is nearly always included in a Thai meal. It is placed on the table alongside the other dishes to be enjoyed a little at a time, as a liquid refreshment as and when each diner chooses.

Thai soups, which are quick and easy to prepare, are usually based on a light broth and many of them are enriched with coconut milk like the Pumpkin and Coconut Soup.

Without doubt the most famous soup is Tom Yam Goong – Hot and Sour Prawn Soup. A symphony of flavour, it uses many local favourites such as lemon grass, galangal, coriander, kaffir lime leaves and, of course, chillies.

Pork and Pickled Mustard Greens Soup

INGREDIENTS

Serves 4–6

225g/8oz pickled mustard leaves, soaked
50g/2oz cellophane noodles, soaked
15ml/1 tbsp vegetable oil
4 garlic cloves, finely sliced
1 litre/1³⁄₄ pints/4 cups chicken stock
450g/1lb pork ribs, cut into large chunks
30ml/2 tbsp fish sauce
pinch of sugar
freshly ground black pepper
2 red chillies, seeded and finely sliced, to garnish

3 Heat the oil in a small frying pan, add the garlic and stir-fry until golden. Transfer the mixture to a bowl and set aside.

4 Put the stock in a saucepan, bring to the boil, then add the pork and simmer gently for 10–15 minutes.

5 Add the pickled mustard leaves and cellophane noodles. Bring back to the boil. Season to taste with fish sauce, sugar and freshly ground black pepper. Serve hot, topped with the fried garlic and red chillies.

1 Cut the pickled mustard leaves into bite-size pieces. Taste to check the seasoning. If they are too salty, then soak them for a little bit longer.

2 Drain the cellophane noodles and cut them into short lengths.

Chiang Mai Noodle Soup

A signature dish of the city of Chiang Mai, this delicious noodle soup has Burmese origins and is the Thai equivalent of the Malaysian 'Laksa'.

INGREDIENTS

Serves 4–6
600ml/1 pint/2½ cups coconut milk
30ml/2 tbsp red curry paste
5ml/1 tsp ground turmeric
450g/1lb chicken thighs, boned and
   cut into bite-size chunks
600ml/1 pint/2½ cups chicken stock
60ml/4 tbsp fish sauce
15ml/1 tbsp dark soy sauce
salt and freshly ground black pepper
juice of ½–1 lime
450g/1lb fresh egg noodles, blanched
   briefly in boiling water

For the garnish
3 spring onions, chopped
4 red chillies, chopped
4 shallots, chopped
60ml/4 tbsp sliced pickled mustard
   leaves, rinsed
30ml/2 tbsp fried sliced garlic
coriander leaves
4 fried noodle nests (optional)

1 In a large saucepan, add about one third of the coconut milk and bring to the boil, stirring often with a wooden spoon until it separates.

2 Add the curry paste and ground turmeric, stir to mix completely and cook until fragrant.

3 Add the chicken and stir-fry for about 2 minutes, ensuring that all the chunks are coated with the paste.

4 Add the remaining coconut milk, chicken stock, fish sauce and soy sauce. Season with salt and freshly ground black pepper to taste. Simmer gently for 7–10 minutes. Remove from the heat and stir in the lime juice.

5 Reheat the noodles in boiling water, drain and divide between individual bowls. Divide the chicken between the bowls and ladle in the hot soup. Top each serving with a few of each of the garnishes.

Ginger, Chicken and Coconut Soup

This aromatic soup is rich with coconut milk and intensely flavoured with galangal, lemon grass and kaffir lime leaves.

INGREDIENTS

Serves 4–6

750ml/1¼ pints/3 cups coconut milk
475ml/16fl oz/2 cups chicken stock
4 stalks lemon grass, bruised
  and chopped
2.5cm/1in piece galangal, thinly sliced
10 black peppercorns, crushed
10 kaffir lime leaves, torn
300g/11oz boneless chicken, cut
  into thin strips
115g/4oz button mushrooms
50g/2oz baby sweetcorn
60ml/4 tbsp lime juice
45ml/3 tbsp fish sauce
2 red chillies, chopped, to garnish
chopped spring onions, to garnish
coriander leaves, to garnish

1 Bring the coconut milk and chicken stock to the boil. Add the lemon grass, galangal, peppercorns and half the kaffir lime leaves, reduce the heat and simmer gently for 10 minutes.

2 Strain the stock into a clean pan. Return to the heat, then add the chicken, button mushrooms and baby sweetcorn. Cook for about 5–7 minutes or until the chicken is cooked.

3 Stir in the lime juice, fish sauce to taste and the rest of the lime leaves. Serve hot, garnished with red chillies, spring onions and coriander.

Hot And Sour Prawn Soup with Lemon Grass

This is a classic Thai seafood soup – *Tom Yam Goong* – and is probably the most popular and well known soup from Thailand.

INGREDIENTS

Serves 4–6

450g/1lb king prawns
1 litre/1¾ pints/4 cups chicken stock
  or water
3 stalks lemon grass
10 kaffir lime leaves, torn in half
225g/8oz can straw mushrooms,
  drained
45ml/3 tbsp fish sauce
50ml/2fl oz/¼ cup lime juice
30ml/2 tbsp chopped spring onion
15ml/1 tbsp coriander leaves
4 red chillies, seeded and chopped
2 spring onions, finely chopped

1 Shell and devein the prawns and set aside. Rinse the prawn shells and place in a large saucepan with the stock or water and bring to the boil.

2 Bruise the lemon grass stalks with the blunt edge of a chopping knife and add them to the stock together with half of the lime leaves. Simmer gently for 5–6 minutes, until the stalks change colour and the stock is fragrant.

3 Strain the stock and return to the saucepan and reheat. Add the mushrooms and prawns, then cook until the prawns turn pink.

4 Stir in the fish sauce, lime juice, spring onions, coriander, red chillies and the rest of the lime leaves. Taste and adjust the seasoning. It should be sour, salty, spicy and hot.

Pumpkin and Coconut Soup

INGREDIENTS

Serves 4–6

2 garlic cloves, crushed
4 shallots, finely chopped
2.5ml/½ tsp shrimp paste
15ml/1 tbsp dried shrimps soaked for
   10 minutes and drained
1 stalk lemon grass, chopped
2 green chillies, seeded
salt, to taste
600ml/1 pint/2½ cups chicken stock
450g/1lb pumpkin, cut into 2cm/¾in
   thick chunks
600ml/1 pint/2½ cups coconut cream
30ml/2 tbsp fish sauce
5ml/1 tsp granulated sugar
115g/4oz small cooked shelled prawns
freshly ground black pepper
2 red chillies, seeded and finely sliced,
   to garnish
10–12 basil leaves, to garnish

1 Grind the garlic, shallots, shrimp paste, dried shrimps, lemon grass, green chillies and salt into a paste.

2 In a large saucepan, bring the chicken stock to the boil, add the ground paste and stir to dissolve.

3 Add the pumpkin and simmer for about 10–15 minutes or until the pumpkin is tender.

4 Stir in the coconut cream, then bring back to a simmer. Add the fish sauce, sugar and ground black pepper to taste.

5 Add the prawns and cook until they are heated through. Serve garnished with the sliced red chillies and basil leaves.

—— COOK'S TIP ——

Shrimp paste, which is made from ground shrimps fermented in brine, is used to give food a savoury flavour.

Spinach and Bean Curd Soup

An extremely delicate and mild-flavoured soup that can be used to counterbalance the heat from a hot Thai curry.

INGREDIENTS

Serves 4–6
30ml/2 tbsp dried shrimps
1 litre/1¾ pints/4 cups chicken stock
225g/8oz fresh bean curd, drained and cut into 2cm/¾in cubes
30ml/2 tbsp fish sauce
350g/12oz fresh spinach, washed thoroughly
freshly ground black pepper
2 spring onions, finely sliced, to garnish

1 Rinse and drain the dried shrimps. Combine the shrimps with the chicken stock in a large saucepan and bring to the boil.

2 Add the bean curd and simmer for about 5 minutes. Season with fish sauce and black pepper to taste.

3 Tear the spinach leaves into bite-size pieces and add to the soup. Cook for another 1–2 minutes.

4 Remove from the heat and sprinkle over the finely sliced with spring onions, to garnish.

--- COOK'S TIP ---

Home-made chicken stock makes the world of difference to clear soups. Whenever you have accumulated enough bones, make a big batch of stock, use what you need and keep the rest in the freezer.

Put 1.5kg/3–3½lb meaty chicken bones and 450g/1lb pork bones (optional) into a large saucepan. Add 3 litres/5 pints/12 cups water and slowly bring to the boil. Occasionally skim off and discard any scum that rises to the surface. Add 2 slices fresh root ginger, 2 garlic cloves (optional), 2 celery sticks, 4 spring onions, 2 bruised lemon grass stalks, a few coriander stalks and 10 crushed black peppercorns. Reduce the heat to low and simmer for about 2–2½ hours. Remove from the heat and leave to cool, uncovered and undisturbed. Pour through a fine strainer, leaving the last dregs behind, as they tend to cloud the soup. Use as required, removing any fat that congeals on the surface.

SALADS AND VEGETABLES

Thai salads are in a class of their own. In preparing a
salad, a Thai cook will always strive for a mix of
colours, contrasting flavours of hot, sweet, sour and
salty, all combined in perfect harmony. Freshly picked
vegetables, aromatic herbs and flavourful leaves are
chopped, sliced, spiced and blended, then topped with
an array of roasted peanuts, crispy fried shallot, garlic
and fresh chillies. When slices of meat and seafood are
included, these salads may well be served as a main
course. Use the freshest of ingredients and taste the
food as you assemble the dish. You may find some
things are too sweet, too sour or too salty to your
palate, so adjust the ingredients to suit your taste.
Vegetables may be stir-fried, steamed or boiled, but
keep the cooking time to a minimum so as to retain all
the flavour and goodness.

Aubergine Salad with Dried Shrimps and Egg

An appetizing and unusual salad that you will find yourself making over and over again.

INGREDIENTS

Serves 4–6
2 aubergines
15ml/1 tbsp oil
30ml/2 tbsp dried shrimps, soaked
  and drained
15ml/1 tbsp coarsely chopped garlic
30ml/2 tbsp freshly squeezed lime juice
5ml/1 tsp palm sugar
30ml/2 tbsp fish sauce
1 hard-boiled egg, shelled and chopped
4 shallots, finely sliced into rings
coriander leaves, to garnish
2 red chillies, seeded and sliced,
  to garnish

—— COOK'S TIP ——

For an interesting variation, try using salted duck's or quail's eggs, cut in half, instead of chopped chicken's eggs.

1 Grill or roast the aubergines until charred and tender.

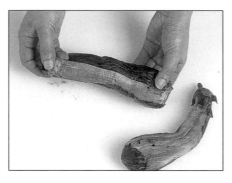

2 When cool enough to handle, peel away the skin and slice the flesh.

3 Heat the oil in a small frying pan, add the drained shrimps and garlic and fry until golden. Remove from the pan and set aside.

4 To make the dressing, put the lime juice, palm sugar and fish sauce in a small bowl and whisk together.

5 To serve, arrange the aubergine on a serving dish. Top with the egg, shallots and dried shrimp mixture. Drizzle over the dressing and garnish with coriander and red chillies.

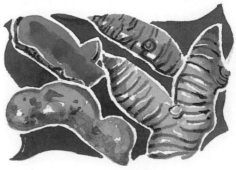

Thai Beef Salad

A hearty salad of beef, laced with a chilli and lime dressing.

INGREDIENTS

Serves 4

2 x 225g/8oz sirloin steaks
1 red onion, finely sliced
½ cucumber, finely sliced into
  matchsticks
1 stalk lemon grass, finely chopped
juice of 2 limes
15–30ml/1–2 tbsp fish sauce
30ml/2 tbsp chopped spring onions
2–4 red chillies, finely sliced, to garnish
fresh coriander, Chinese mustard cress
  and mint leaves, to garnish

1 Pan-fry or grill the beef steaks to medium-rare. Allow to rest for 10–15 minutes.

2 When cool, thinly slice the beef and put the slices in a large bowl.

3 Add the sliced onion, cucumber matchsticks and lemon grass.

4 Add the spring onions. Toss and season with lime juice and fish sauce. Serve at room temperature or chilled, garnished with the chillies, coriander, mustard cress and mint.

Larp of Chiang Mai

Chiang Mai is a city in the north-east of Thailand. The city is culturally very close to Laos and famous for its chicken salad, which was originally called 'Laap' or 'Larp'. Duck, beef or pork can be used instead of chicken.

INGREDIENTS

Serves 4–6
450g/1lb minced chicken
1 stalk lemon grass, finely chopped
3 kaffir lime leaves, finely chopped
4 red chillies, seeded and chopped
60ml/4 tbsp lime juice
30ml/2 tbsp fish sauce
15ml/1 tbsp roasted ground rice
2 spring onions, chopped
30ml/2 tbsp coriander leaves
mixed salad leaves, cucumber and
    tomato slices, to serve
a few sprigs of mint, to garnish

1 Heat a large non-stick frying pan. Add the minced chicken and cook in a little water.

COOK'S TIP

Use sticky, or glutinous, rice to make roasted ground rice. Put the rice in a frying pan and dry-roast until golden brown. Remove and grind to a powder in a pestle and mortar or in a food processor. Keep in a glass jar in a cool and dry place and use as required.

2 Stir constantly until cooked; this will take about 7–10 minutes.

3 Transfer the cooked chicken to a large bowl and add the rest of the ingredients. Mix thoroughly.

4 Serve on a bed of mixed salad leaves, cucumber and tomato slices and garnish with sprigs of mint.

Tangy Chicken Salad

This fresh and lively dish typifies the character of Thai cuisine. It is ideal for a starter or light lunch.

INGREDIENTS

Serves 4–6

4 skinned, boneless chicken breasts
2 garlic cloves, crushed and
  roughly chopped
30ml/2 tbsp soy sauce
30ml/2 tbsp vegetable oil
120ml/4fl oz/½ cup coconut cream
30ml/2 tbsp fish sauce
juice of 1 lime
30ml/2 tbsp palm sugar
115g/4oz water chestnuts, sliced
50g/2oz cashew nuts, roasted
4 shallots, finely sliced
4 kaffir lime leaves, finely sliced
1 stalk lemon grass, finely sliced
5ml/1 tsp chopped galangal
1 large red chilli, seeded and
  finely sliced
2 spring onions, finely sliced
10–12 mint leaves, torn
1 head of lettuce, to serve
sprigs of coriander, to garnish
2 red chillies, seeded and sliced,
  to garnish

1 Trim the chicken breasts of any excess fat and put them in a large dish. Rub with the garlic, soy sauce and 15ml/1 tbsp of the oil. Leave to marinate for 1–2 hours.

2 Grill or pan-fry the chicken for 3–4 minutes on both sides or until cooked. Remove and set aside to cool.

3 In a small saucepan, heat the coconut cream, fish sauce, lime juice and palm sugar. Stir until all of the sugar has dissolved and then remove from the heat.

4 Cut the cooked chicken into strips and combine with the water chestnuts, cashew nuts, shallots, kaffir lime leaves, lemon grass, galangal, red chilli, spring onions and mint leaves.

5 Pour the coconut dressing over the chicken, toss and mix well. Serve the chicken on a bed of lettuce leaves and garnish with sprigs of coriander and sliced red chillies.

Seafood Salad with Fragrant Herbs

INGREDIENTS
Serves 4–6

250ml/8fl oz/1 cup fish stock or water
350g/12oz squid, cleaned and cut
   into rings
12 uncooked king prawns, shelled
12 scallops
50g/2oz bean thread noodles, soaked
   in warm water for 30 minutes
½ cucumber, cut into thin sticks
1 stalk lemon grass, finely chopped
2 kaffir lime leaves, finely shredded
2 shallots, finely sliced
juice of 1–2 limes
30ml/2 tbsp fish sauce
30ml/2 tbsp chopped spring onion
30ml/2 tbsp coriander leaves
12–15 mint leaves, roughly torn
4 red chillies, sliced
sprigs of coriander, to garnish

1 Pour the stock or water into a medium-size saucepan, set over a high heat and bring to the boil.

2 Cook each type of seafood separately in the stock for a few minutes. Remove and set aside.

3 Drain the bean thread noodles and cut them into short lengths, about 5cm/2in long. Combine the noodles with the cooked seafood.

4 Add all the remaining ingredients, mix together well and serve garnished with the coriander sprigs.

Pomelo Salad

Pomelo is a large fruit that resembles a grapefruit. It has a much sturdier and drier flesh.

INGREDIENTS

Serves 4–6
For the dressing
30ml/2 tbsp fish sauce
15ml/1 tbsp palm sugar
30ml/2 tbsp lime juice

For the salad
30ml/2 tbsp vegetable oil
4 shallots, finely sliced
2 garlic cloves, finely sliced
1 large pomelo
115g/4oz cooked shelled prawns
115g/4oz cooked crab meat
15ml/1 tbsp roasted peanuts
10–12 small mint leaves
2 spring onions, finely sliced
2 red chillies, seeded and finely sliced
coriander leaves, to garnish
shredded fresh coconut (optional)

1 Whisk together the fish sauce, palm sugar and lime juice and set aside.

2 Heat the oil in a small frying pan, add the shallots and garlic and fry until they are golden. Remove from the pan and set aside.

3 Peel the pomelo and break the flesh into small pieces, taking care to remove any membranes.

4 Coarsely grind the peanuts, then combine with the pomelo flesh, prawns, crab meat, mint leaves and the fried shallot mixture. Toss in the dressing and serve sprinkled with the spring onions, red chillies, coriander leaves and shredded coconut, if using.

Cabbage Salad

A simple and delicious way of using cabbage. Other vegetables such as broccoli, cauliflower, beansprouts and Chinese cabbage can also be prepared this way.

INGREDIENTS

Serves 4–6
30ml/2 tbsp fish sauce
grated rind of 1 lime
30ml/2 tbsp lime juice
120ml/4fl oz/½ cup coconut milk
30ml/2 tbsp vegetable oil
2 large red chillies, seeded and finely
    cut into strips
6 garlic cloves, finely sliced
6 shallots, finely sliced
1 small cabbage, shredded
30ml/2 tbsp coarsely chopped roasted
    peanuts, to serve

1 Make the dressing by combining the fish sauce, lime rind and juice and coconut milk. Set aside.

2 Heat the oil in a wok or frying pan. Stir-fry the chillies, garlic and shallots, until the shallots are brown and crisp. Remove and set aside.

3 Blanch the cabbage in boiling salted water for about 2–3 minutes, drain and put into a bowl.

4 Stir the dressing into the cabbage, toss and mix well. Transfer the salad into a serving dish. Sprinkle with the fried shallot mixture and the chopped roasted peanuts.

Bamboo Shoot Salad

This salad, which has a hot and sharp flavour, originated in north-east Thailand. Use fresh young bamboo shoots when you can find them, otherwise substitute canned bamboo shoots.

INGREDIENTS

Serves 4

400g/14oz can whole bamboo shoots
25g/1oz glutinous rice
30ml/2 tbsp chopped shallots
15ml/1 tbsp chopped garlic
45ml/3 tbsp chopped spring onions
30ml/2 tbsp fish sauce
30ml/2 tbsp lime juice
5ml/1 tsp granulated sugar
2.5ml/½ tsp dried flaked chillies
20–25 small mint leaves
15ml/1 tbsp toasted sesame seeds

3 Tip the rice into a bowl, add the shallots, garlic, spring onions, fish sauce, lime juice, granulated sugar, chillies and half the mint leaves.

4 Mix thoroughly, then pour over the bamboo shoots and toss together. Serve sprinkled with sesame seeds and the remaining mint leaves.

1 Rinse and drain the bamboo shoots, finely slice and set aside.

2 Dry roast the rice in a frying pan until it is golden brown. Remove and grind to fine crumbs with a pestle and mortar.

Stir-fried Beansprouts

Sprouted from mung beans, beansprouts have a delicate taste, they are very nutritious and also easy to digest. They are widely available in most supermarkets.

INGREDIENTS

Serves 4–6
30ml/2 tbsp oil
2 garlic cloves, chopped
15ml/1 tbsp dried shrimp, soaked and rinsed
115g/4 oz minced lean pork
250g/8oz beansprouts
115/4oz garlic chives, chopped
15ml/1 tbsp fish sauce
5ml/1 tsp caster sugar
freshly ground black pepper
coriander leaves, to garnish

1 Heat the oil in a wok or deep frying pan. Add the garlic and dried shrimps and fry until golden.

2 Add the pork and fry over a high heat for 3–5 minutes or until the pork is cooked.

3 Add the beansprouts, garlic chives, fish sauce, sugar and pepper. Serve garnished with coriander leaves.

COOK'S TIP

If you like, you can use minced chicken or beef instead of pork. For a vegetarian version, substitute fried beancurd.

Green Papaya Salad

There are many variations of this salad in south-east Asia. As green papaya is not easy to get hold of, shredded carrots, cucumber or green apple may also be used. Serve this salad with raw Chinese or white cabbage and rice.

INGREDIENTS

Serves 4
1 medium-size green papaya
4 garlic cloves
15ml/1 tbsp chopped shallot
3–4 red chillies, seeded and sliced
2.5ml/½ tsp salt
2–3 snake beans (or green or runner beans), cut into 2cm/¾in lengths
2 tomatoes, cut into wedges
45ml/3 tbsp fish sauce
15ml/1 tbsp caster sugar
juice of 1 lime
30ml/2 tbsp crushed roasted peanuts
sliced red chillies, to garnish

1 Peel the papaya and cut in half lengthways, scrape out the seeds with a spoon and finely shred the flesh.

COOK'S TIP

If you do not have a large pestle and mortar, use a bowl and crush the shredded papaya with a wooden meat tenderizer or the end of a rolling pin.

---

2 Grind the garlic, shallots, chillies and salt together in a large mortar with a pestle.

3 Add the shredded papaya a little at a time and pound until it becomes a little limp and soft.

4 Add the sliced beans and tomatoes and lightly crush. Season with fish sauce, sugar and lime juice.

5 Transfer the salad to a serving dish, sprinkle with crushed peanuts and garnish with the red chillies.

Water Spinach with Brown Bean Sauce

Water spinach, often known as Siamese watercress, is a green vegetable with arrowhead-shaped leaves. If you can't find it, use spinach, watercress, pak choy or even broccoli, and adjust the cooking time accordingly. There are excellent variations to this recipe using black bean sauce, shrimp paste or fermented bean curd instead of brown bean sauce.

INGREDIENTS

Serves 4–6

1 bunch water spinach, about
   1kg/2¼lb in weight
45ml/3 tbsp vegetable oil
15ml/1 tbsp chopped garlic
15ml/1 tbsp brown bean sauce
30ml/2 tbsp fish sauce
15ml/1 tbsp granulated sugar
freshly black ground pepper

1 Trim and discard the bottom coarse, woody end of the water spinach. Cut the remaining part into 5cm/2in lengths, keeping the leaves separate from the stems.

2 Heat the oil in a wok or large frying pan. When it starts to smoke, add the chopped garlic and toss for 10 seconds.

3 Add the stem part of the water spinach, let it sizzle and cook for 1 minute, then add the leafy parts.

4 Stir in the brown bean sauce, fish sauce, sugar and pepper. Toss and turn over the spinach until it begins to wilt, about 3–4 minutes. Transfer to a serving dish and serve immediately.

Mixed Vegetables in Coconut Milk

A most delicious way of cooking vegetables. If you don't like highly spiced food, use fewer red chilli peppers.

INGREDIENTS

Serves 4–6

450g/1lb mixed vegetables, such as
   aubergines, baby sweetcorn, carrots,
   snake beans and patty pan squash
8 red chillies, seeded
2 stalks lemon grass, chopped
4 kaffir lime leaves, torn
30ml/2 tbsp vegetable oil
250ml/8fl oz/1 cup coconut milk
30ml/2 tbsp fish sauce
salt
15–20 Thai basil leaves, to garnish

1 Cut the vegetables into similar size shapes using a sharp knife.

2 Put the red chillies, lemon grass and kaffir lime leaves in a mortar and grind together with a pestle.

3 Heat the oil in a wok or large deep frying pan. Add the chilli mixture and fry for 2–3 minutes.

4 Stir in the coconut milk and bring to the boil. Add the vegetables and cook for about 5 minutes or until they are tender. Season with the fish sauce and salt, and garnish with basil leaves

MAIN COURSES

*Thailand has a tropical cornucopia of good things to eat
and its coastal regions yield an abundance of seafood,
both tempting and exotic.*

*Thais do not divide meals into courses as Westerners
do; instead all the dishes are brought out and served at
once. In a typical meal there will be a compilation of
four to five different dishes with contrasting textures and
flavours. These dishes will nearly always include a clear
soup, different meats, seafood and vegetable dishes that
are fried or steamed, a curry, a salad, one or two hot
sauces and, of course, rice.*

*There should be no duplication or repetition and
ingredients and colours should be as diverse as possible.
This reflects the influence of the Chinese principle of
ying and yang; the idea is to achieve overall healthful
harmony by balancing opposing qualities.*

Satay Prawns

An enticing and tasty dish. Serve with greens and jasmine rice.

INGREDIENTS

Serves 4–6

450g/1lb king prawns, shelled, tail ends
   left intact and deveined
½ bunch coriander leaves, to garnish
4 red chillies, finely sliced, to garnish
spring onions, cut diagonally, to garnish

For the peanut sauce

45ml/3 tbsp vegetable oil
15ml/1 tbsp chopped garlic
1 small onion, chopped
3–4 red chillies, crushed and chopped
3 kaffir lime leaves, torn
1 stalk lemon grass, bruised
   and chopped
5ml/1 tsp medium curry paste
250ml/8fl oz/1 cup coconut milk
1.5cm/½in cinnamon stick
75g/3oz crunchy peanut butter
45ml/3 tbsp tamarind juice
30ml/2 tbsp fish sauce
30ml/2 tbsp palm sugar
juice of ½ lemon

1 To make the sauce, heat half the oil in a wok or large frying pan and add the garlic and onion. Cook until it softens, about 3–4 minutes.

2 Add the chillies, kaffir lime leaves, lemon grass and curry paste. Cook for a further 2–3 minutes.

COOK'S TIP

Curry paste has a far superior, authentic flavour to powdered varieties. Once opened, they should be kept in the fridge and used within 2 months.

3 Stir in the coconut milk, cinnamon stick, peanut butter, tamarind juice, fish sauce, palm sugar and lemon juice.

4 Reduce the heat and simmer gently for 15–20 minutes until the sauce thickens, stirring occasionally to ensure the sauce doesn't stick to the bottom of the wok or frying pan.

5 Heat the rest of the oil in a wok or large frying pan. Add the prawns and stir-fry for about 3–4 minutes or until the prawns turn pink and are slightly firm to the touch.

6 Mix the prawns with the sauce. Serve garnished with coriander leaves, red chillies and spring onions.

Sweet and Sour Fish

When fish is cooked in this way the skin becomes crispy on the outside, while the flesh remains moist and juicy inside. The sweet and sour sauce, with its colourful cherry tomatoes, complements the fish beautifully.

INGREDIENTS

Serves 4–6

1 large or 2 medium-size fish such as
   snapper or mullet, heads removed
20ml/4 tsp cornflour
120ml/4fl oz/½ cup vegetable oil
15ml/1 tbsp chopped garlic
15ml/1 tbsp chopped root ginger
30ml/2 tbsp chopped shallots
225g/8oz cherry tomatoes
30ml/2 tbsp red wine vinegar
30ml/2 tbsp granulated sugar
30ml/2 tbsp tomato ketchup
15ml/1 tbsp fish sauce
45ml/3 tbsp water
salt and freshly ground black pepper
coriander leaves, to garnish
shredded spring onions, to garnish

1 Thoroughly rinse and clean the fish. Score the skin diagonally on both sides of the fish.

2 Coat the fish lightly on both sides with 15ml/1 tbsp cornflour. Shake off any excess.

3 Heat the oil in a wok or large frying pan and slide the fish into the wok. Reduce the heat to medium and fry the fish until crisp and brown, about 6–7 minutes on both sides.

4 Remove the fish with a fish slice and place on a large platter.

5 Pour off all but 30ml/2 tbsp of the oil and add the garlic, ginger and shallots. Fry until golden.

6 Add the cherry tomatoes and cook until they burst open. Stir in the vinegar, sugar, tomato ketchup and fish sauce. Simmer gently for 1–2 minutes and adjust the seasoning.

7 Blend the remaining 5ml/1 tsp cornflour with the water. Stir into the sauce and heat until it thickens. Pour the sauce over the fish and garnish with coriander leaves and shredded spring onions.

Baked Fish in Banana Leaves

Fish that is prepared in this way is particularly succulent and flavourful. Fillets are used here rather than whole fish – easier for those who don't like to mess about with bones. It is a great dish for outdoor barbecues.

INGREDIENTS

Serves 4

250ml/8fl oz/1 cup coconut milk
30ml/2 tbsp red curry paste
45ml/3 tbsp fish sauce
30ml/2 tbsp caster sugar
5 kaffir lime leaves, torn
4 x 175g/6oz fish fillets, such as snapper
175g/6oz mixed vegetables, such as carrots or leeks, finely shredded
4 banana leaves
30ml/2 tbsp shredded spring onions, to garnish
2 red chillies, finely sliced, to garnish

1 Combine the coconut milk, curry paste, fish sauce, sugar and kaffir lime leaves in a shallow dish.

2 Marinate the fish in this mixture for about 15–30 minutes. Preheat the oven to 200°C/400°F/Gas 6.

3 Mix the vegetables together and lay a portion on top of a banana leaf. Place a piece of fish on top with a little of its marinade.

4 Wrap the fish up by turning in the sides and ends of the leaf and secure with cocktail sticks. Repeat with the rest of the leaves and fish.

5 Bake in the hot oven for 20–25 minutes or until the fish is cooked. Alternatively, cook under the grill or on the barbeque. Just before serving, garnish the fish with a sprinkling of spring onions and sliced red chillies.

Stir-fried Scallops with Asparagus

Asparagus is extremely popular among the Chinese Thai. The combination of garlic and black pepper gives this dish its spiciness. You can substitute the scallops with prawns or other firm fish.

INGREDIENTS

Serves 4–6

60ml/4 tbsp vegetable oil
1 bunch asparagus, cut into 5cm/2in lengths
4 garlic cloves, finely chopped
2 shallots, finely chopped
450g/1lb scallops, cleaned
30ml/2 tbsp fish sauce
2.5ml/½ tsp coarsely ground black pepper
120ml/4fl oz/½ cup coconut milk
coriander leaves, to garnish

1 Heat half the oil in a wok or large frying pan. Add the asparagus and stir-fry for about 2 minutes. Transfer the asparagus to a plate and set aside.

2 Add the rest of the oil, garlic and shallots to the same wok and fry until fragrant. Add the scallops and cook for another 1–2 minutes.

3 Return the asparagus to the wok. Add the fish sauce, black pepper and coconut milk.

4 Stir and cook for another 3–4 minutes or until the scallops and asparagus are cooked. Garnish with the coriander leaves.

Steamed Fish with Chilli Sauce

Steaming is one of the best methods of cooking fish. By leaving the fish whole and on the bone, you'll find that all the flavour and moistness is retained.

INGREDIENTS

Serves 4

1 large or 2 medium firm fish like bass
or grouper, scaled and cleaned
1 fresh banana leaf
30ml/2 tbsp rice wine
3 red chillies, seeded and finely sliced
2 garlic cloves, finely chopped
2cm/³/₄in piece fresh root ginger,
finely shredded
2 stalks lemon grass, crushed
and finely chopped
2 spring onions, chopped
30ml/2 tbsp fish sauce
juice of 1 lime

For the chilli sauce

10 red chillies, seeded and chopped
4 garlic cloves, chopped
60 ml/4 tbsp fish sauce
15ml/1 tbsp sugar
75ml/5 tbsp lime juice

1 Rinse the fish under cold running water. Pat dry with kitchen paper. With a sharp knife, slash the skin of the fish a few times on both sides.

2 Place the fish on a banana leaf. Mix together all the remaining ingredients and spread over the fish.

3 Place a small upturned plate in the bottom of a wok and add 5cm/2in boiling water; place a banana leaf on top. Lift the banana leaf, together with the fish, and place on the plate or rack. Cover with a lid and steam for about 10–15 minutes or until the fish is cooked.

4 Place all the chilli sauce ingredients in a food processor and process until smooth. You may need to add a little cold water.

5 Serve the fish hot, on the banana leaf if liked, with the sweet chilli sauce to spoon over the top.

Stir-fried Prawns with Tamarind

The sour, tangy flavour that is characteristic of many Thai dishes comes from tamarind. Fresh tamarind pods from the tamarind tree can sometimes be bought, but preparing them for cooking is a laborious process. The Thais, however, usually prefer to use compressed blocks of tamarind paste, which is simply soaked in warm water and then strained.

INGREDIENTS

Serves 4–6
50g/2oz tamarind paste
150ml/¼ pint/⅔ cup boiling water
30ml/2 tbsp vegetable oil
30ml/2 tbsp chopped onion
30ml/2 tbsp palm sugar
30ml/2 tbsp chicken stock or water
15ml/1 tbsp fish sauce
6 dried red chillies, fried
450g/1lb uncooked shelled prawns
15ml/1 tbsp fried chopped garlic
30ml/2 tbsp fried sliced shallots
2 spring onions, chopped, to garnish

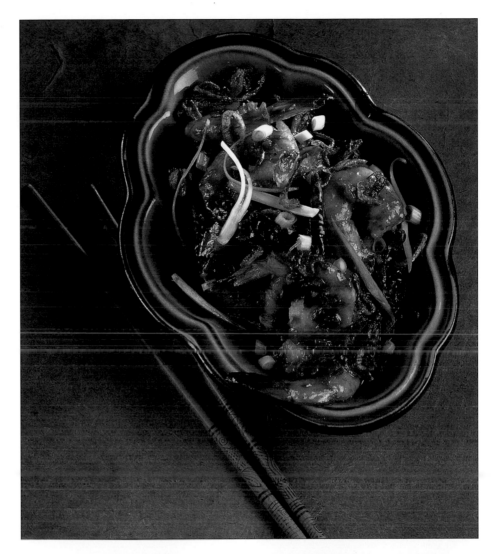

1 Put the tamarind paste in a small bowl, pour over the boiling water and stir well to break up any lumps. Leave for 30 minutes. Strain, pushing as much of the juice through as possible. Measure 90ml/6 tbsp of the juice, the amount needed, and store the remainder in the fridge. Heat the oil in a wok. Add the chopped onion and fry until golden brown.

2 Add the sugar, stock, fish sauce, dried chillies and the tamarind juice, stirring well until the sugar dissolves. Bring to the boil.

3 Add the prawns, garlic and shallots. Stir-fry until the prawns are cooked, about 3–4 minutes. Garnish with the spring onions.

Chicken Livers, Thai-style

Chicken liver is a good source of iron and is a popular meat, especially in the north-east of Thailand. Serve this dish as a starter with salad, or as part of a main course with jasmine rice.

INGREDIENTS

Serves 4–6

45ml/3 tbsp vegetable oil
450g/1lb chicken livers, trimmed
4 shallots, chopped
2 garlic cloves, chopped
15ml/1 tbsp roasted ground rice
45ml/3 tbsp fish sauce
45ml/3 tbsp lime juice
5ml/1 tsp sugar
2 stalks lemon grass, bruised and finely chopped
30ml/2 tbsp chopped coriander
10–12 mint leaves, to garnish
2 red chillies, chopped, to garnish

1 Heat the oil in a wok or large frying pan. Add the livers and fry over a medium-high heat for about 4 minutes, until the liver is golden brown and cooked, but still pink inside.

2 Move the liver to one side of the pan and add the shallots and garlic. Fry for about 1–2 minutes.

3 Add the roasted ground rice, fish sauce, lime juice, sugar, lemon grass and coriander. Stir to combine. Remove from the heat and serve garnished with mint leaves and chillies.

Barbecued Chicken

Barbecued chicken is served almost everywhere in Thailand, from portable roadside stalls to sports stadiums and beaches.

INGREDIENTS

Serves 4–6

1 chicken, about 1.5kg/3–3½ lb, cut into 8–10 pieces
2 limes, cut into wedges, to garnish
2 red chillies, finely sliced, to garnish

For the marinade

2 stalks lemon grass, chopped
2.5cm/1in piece fresh root ginger
6 garlic cloves
4 shallots
½ bunch coriander roots
15ml/1 tbsp palm sugar
120ml/4fl oz/½ cup coconut milk
30ml/2 tbsp fish sauce
30ml/2 tbsp soy sauce

1 To make the marinade, put all the ingredients into a food processor and process until smooth.

2 Put the chicken pieces in a dish and pour over the marinade. Leave in a cool place to marinate for at least 4 hours or overnight.

3 Barbecue the chicken over glowing coals, or place on a rack over a baking tray and bake at 200°C/400°F/ Gas 6 for about 20–30 minutes or until the chicken is cooked and golden brown. Turn the pieces occasionally and brush with the marinade.

4 Garnish with lime wedges and finely sliced red chillies.

Cashew Chicken

In this Chinese-inspired dish, tender pieces of chicken are stir-fried with cashew nuts, red chillies and a touch of garlic, for a delicious combination.

Ingredients

Serves 4–6

450g/1lb boneless chicken breasts
30ml/2 tbsp vegetable oil
2 garlic cloves, sliced
4 dried red chillies, chopped
1 red pepper, seeded and cut into
   2cm/¾in dice
30ml/2 tbsp oyster sauce
15ml/1 tbsp soy sauce
pinch of granulated sugar
1 bunch spring onions, cut into
   5cm/2in lengths
175g/6oz cashew nuts, roasted
coriander leaves, to garnish

1 Remove and discard the skin from the chicken breasts. With a sharp knife, cut the chicken into bite-size pieces and set aside.

2 Heat the oil in a wok and swirl it around. Add the garlic and dried chillies and fry until golden.

3 Add the chicken and stir-fry until it changes colour, then add the red pepper. If necessary, add a little water.

4 Stir in the oyster sauce, soy sauce and sugar. Add the spring onions and cashew nuts. Stir-fry for about another 1–2 minutes. Serve garnished with coriander leaves.

Stir-fried Chicken with Basil and Chillies

This quick and easy chicken dish is an excellent introduction to Thai cuisine. Deep frying the basil adds another dimension to this dish. Thai basil, which is sometimes known as Holy basil, has a unique, pungent flavour that is both spicy and sharp. The dull leaves have serrated edges.

INGREDIENTS

Serves 4–6
45ml/3 tbsp vegetable oil
4 garlic cloves, sliced
2–4 red chillies, seeded and chopped
450g/1lb chicken, cut into
  bite-size pieces
30–45ml/2–3 tbsp fish sauce
10ml/2 tsp dark soy sauce
5ml/1 tsp sugar
10–12 Thai basil leaves
2 red chillies, finely sliced, to garnish
20 Thai basil leaves, deep fried
  (optional)

1 Heat the oil in a wok or large frying pan and swirl it around.

2 Add the garlic and chillies and stir-fry until golden.

3 Add the chicken and stir-fry until it changes colour.

4 Season with fish sauce, soy sauce and sugar. Continue to stir-fry for 3-4 minutes or until the chicken is cooked. Stir in the fresh Thai basil leaves. Garnish with sliced chillies and the deep fried basil, if using.

COOK'S TIP

To deep fry Thai basil leaves, make sure that the leaves are completely dry. Deep fry in hot oil for about 30–40 seconds, lift out and drain on kitchen paper.

Fragrant Thai Meatballs

Ingredients

Serves 4–6

450g/1lb lean minced pork or beef
15ml/1 tbsp chopped garlic
1 stalk lemon grass, finely chopped
4 spring onions, finely chopped
15ml/1 tbsp chopped fresh coriander
30ml/2 tbsp red curry paste
15ml/1 tbsp lemon juice
15ml/1 tbsp fish sauce
1 egg
salt and freshly ground black pepper
rice flour for dusting
oil for frying
sprigs of coriander, to garnish

For the peanut sauce

15ml/1 tbsp vegetable oil
15ml/1 tbsp red curry paste
30ml/2 tbsp crunchy peanut butter
15ml/1 tbsp palm sugar
15ml/1 tbsp lemon juice
250ml/8fl oz/1 cup coconut milk

1 Make the peanut sauce. Heat the oil in a small saucepan, add the curry paste and fry for 1 minute.

2 Stir in the rest of the ingredients and bring to the boil. Lower the heat and simmer for 5 minutes, until the sauce thickens.

3 Make the meatballs. Combine all the ingredients except for the rice flour, oil and coriander, and add some seasoning. Mix and blend everything together well.

4 Roll and shape the meat into small balls about the size of a walnut. Dust the meatballs with rice flour.

5 Heat the oil in a wok until hot and deep fry the meatballs in batches until nicely browned and cooked through. Drain on kitchen paper. Serve garnished with sprigs of coriander and accompanied with the peanut sauce.

Stuffed Thai Omelette

Ingredients

Serves 4

30ml/2 tbsp vegetable oil
2 garlic cloves, finely chopped
1 small onion, finely chopped
225g/8oz minced pork
30ml/2 tbsp fish sauce
5ml/1 tsp granulated sugar
freshly ground black pepper
2 tomatoes, peeled and chopped
15ml/1 tbsp chopped fresh coriander

For the omelette

5–6 eggs
15ml/1 tbsp fish sauce
30ml/2 tbsp vegetable oil
sprigs of coriander, to garnish
red chillies, sliced, to garnish

1 First heat the oil in a wok or frying pan. Add the garlic and onion and fry for 3–4 minutes until softened. Stir in the pork and fry for about 7–10 minutes, until lightly browned.

2 Add the fish sauce, sugar, freshly ground pepper and tomatoes. Stir to combine and simmer until the sauce thickens slightly. Mix in the chopped fresh coriander.

3 To make the omelettes, whisk together the eggs and fish sauce.

4 Heat 15ml/1 tbsp of the oil in an omelette pan or wok. Add half the beaten egg and tilt the pan to spread the egg into a thin even sheet.

5 When set, spoon half the filling over the centre of the omelette. Fold in opposite sides; first the top and bottom, then the right and left sides to make a neat square parcel.

6 Slide out on to a warm serving dish, folded-side down. Repeat with the rest of the oil, eggs and filling. Serve garnished with sprigs of coriander and red chillies.

Sweet and Sour Pork, Thai-style

Sweet and sour is traditionally a Chinese creation but the Thais do it very well. This version has an altogether fresher and cleaner flavour and it makes a good one-dish meal when served over rice.

INGREDIENTS

Serves 4
350g/12oz lean pork
30ml/2 tbsp vegetable oil
4 garlic cloves, finely sliced
1 small red onion, sliced
30ml/2 tbsp fish sauce
15ml/1 tbsp granulated sugar
1 red pepper, seeded and diced
½ cucumber, seeded and sliced
2 plum tomatoes, cut into wedges
115g/4oz pineapple, cut into
  small chunks
freshly ground black pepper
2 spring onions, cut into short lengths
coriander leaves, to garnish
spring onions, shredded, to garnish

1 Slice the pork into thin strips. Heat the oil in a wok or large frying pan.

2 Add the garlic and fry until golden, then add the pork and stir-fry for about 4–5 minutes. Add the onion.

3 Season with fish sauce, sugar and freshly ground black pepper. Stir and cook for 3–4 minutes, or until the pork is cooked.

4 Add the rest of the vegetables, the pineapple and spring onions. You may need to add a few tablespoons of water. Continue to stir-fry for another 3–4 minutes. Serve hot garnished with coriander leaves and spring onion.

Lemon Grass Pork Chops with Field Mushrooms

This is a favourite recipe for a barbecue. The enticing aroma of the sizzling meat on the grill makes it popular with everyone.

INGREDIENTS

Serves 4
4 pork chops
4 large field mushrooms
45ml/3 tbsp vegetable oil
4 red chillies, seeded and finely sliced
45ml/3 tbsp fish sauce
90ml/6 tbsp lime juice
4 shallots, chopped
5ml/1 tsp roasted ground rice
30ml/2 tbsp spring onions, chopped
coriander leaves, to garnish
a few spring onions, shredded, to garnish

For the marinade
2 garlic cloves, chopped
15ml/1 tbsp sugar
15ml/1 tbsp fish sauce
30ml/2 tbsp soy sauce
15ml/1 tbsp sesame oil
15ml/1 tbsp whisky or dry sherry
2 stalks lemon grass, finely chopped
2 spring onions, chopped

1 To make the marinade, mix together all the marinade ingredients.

2 Pour over the pork chops and leave to marinate for 1–2 hours.

3 Place the mushrooms and marinated pork chops on a grill pan and brush with 15ml/1 tbsp of the oil. Grill the pork chops for 5–7 minutes on each side and the mushrooms for about 2 minutes. Brush both with the marinade while grilling.

4 Meanwhile heat the rest of the oil in a small frying pan, then remove from the heat and mix in the remaining ingredients. Put the pork chops and mushrooms on a serving plate and spoon over the sauce. Garnish with coriander and shredded spring onion.

Savoury Pork Ribs with Snake Beans

This is a rich and pungent dish. If snake beans are hard to find, you can substitute fine green or runner beans.

INGREDIENTS

Serves 4–6
675g/1½lb pork spare ribs or belly of pork
30ml/2 tbsp vegetable oil
120ml/4fl oz/½ cup water
15ml/1 tbsp palm sugar
15ml/1 tbsp fish sauce
150g/5oz snake beans, cut into 5cm/2in lengths
2 kaffir lime leaves, finely sliced
2 red chillies, finely sliced, to garnish

For the chilli paste
3 dried red chillies, seeded and soaked
4 shallots, chopped
4 garlic cloves, chopped
5ml/1 tsp chopped galangal
1 stalk lemon grass, chopped
6 black peppercorns
5ml/1 tsp shrimp paste
30ml/2 tbsp dried shrimp, rinsed

1 Put all the ingredients for the chilli paste in a mortar and grind together with a pestle until it forms a thick paste.

2 Slice and chop the spare ribs (or belly pork) into 4cm/1½in lengths.

3 Heat the oil in a wok or frying pan. Add the pork and fry for about 5 minutes, until lightly browned.

4 Stir in the chilli paste and continue to cook for another 5 minutes, stirring constantly to stop the paste from sticking to the pan.

5 Add the water, cover and simmer for 7–10 minutes or until the spare ribs are tender. Season with palm sugar and fish sauce.

6 Mix in the snake beans and kaffir lime leaves and fry until the beans are cooked. Serve garnished with sliced red chillies.

Stir-fried Beef in Oyster Sauce

Another simple but delicious recipe. In Thailand fresh straw mushrooms are readily available, but oyster mushrooms make a good substitute. To make the dish even more interesting, use several types of mushroom.

INGREDIENTS

Serves 4–6

450g/1lb rump steak
30ml/2 tbsp soy sauce
15ml/1 tbsp cornflour
45ml/3 tbsp vegetable oil
15ml/1 tbsp chopped garlic
15ml/1 tbsp chopped root ginger
225g/8oz mixed mushrooms such as shiitake, oyster and straw
30ml/2 tbsp oyster sauce
5ml/1 tsp granulated sugar
4 spring onions, cut into short lengths
freshly ground black pepper
2 red chillies, cut into strips, to garnish

1 Slice the beef, on the diagonal, into long thin strips. Mix together the soy sauce and cornflour in a large bowl, stir in the beef and leave to marinate for 1–2 hours.

COOK'S TIP

Made from extracts of oysters, oyster sauce is velvety smooth and has a savoury sweet and meaty taste. There are several types available; buy the best you can afford.

2 Heat half the oil in a wok or frying pan. Add the garlic and ginger and fry until fragrant. Stir in the beef. Stir to separate the strips, let them colour and cook for 1–2 minutes. Remove from the pan and set aside.

3 Heat the remaining oil in the wok. Add the shiitake, oyster and straw mushrooms. Cook until tender.

4 Return the beef to the wok with the mushrooms. Add the oyster sauce, sugar and freshly ground black pepper to taste. Mix well.

5 Add the spring onions. Mix together. Serve garnished with strips of red chilli.

Steamed Eggs with Beef and Spring Onions

This is a very delicate dish. You can add less liquid for a firmer custard, but cooked this way it is soft and silky. Other types of meat or seafood can be used instead of beef.

INGREDIENTS

Serves 4–6

115g/4oz sirloin or rump steak
5ml/1 tsp grated fresh root ginger
15ml/1 tbsp fish sauce
freshly ground black pepper
3 eggs
120ml/4fl oz/½ cup chicken stock
   or water
30ml/2 tbsp chopped spring onion
15ml/1 tbsp vegetable oil
2 garlic cloves, finely sliced

1 Finely chop the beef and place in a large bowl. Add the ginger, fish sauce and freshly ground black pepper.

2 Beat the eggs together with the stock. Stir the mixture into the beef, add the spring onions and beat together until well-blended. Try to avoid making too many bubbles.

3 Pour the mixture into a heatproof dish or individual ramekins.

4 Place in a steamer and steam over a gentle heat for 10–15 minutes or until the custard is set.

5 Meanwhile, heat the oil in a frying pan. Add the garlic and stir to break up any clumps and fry until golden – about 2 minutes.

6 To serve, pour the garlic and oil over the egg custards. Allow to cool slightly before serving.

COOK'S TIP

The Japanese make a similar version of this recipe called *Chewan Mushi*, using spinach, prawns and shiitake mushrooms.

CURRIES

All curry-making begins with the curry paste. In days gone by, each household would have their own recipes, handed down from generation to generation. Various herbs and spices are used, such as lemon grass, kaffir lime leaves, chillies, galangal, coriander and other flavourings. Everything is crushed with a pestle and mortar, resulting in an aromatic and fragrant wet paste, which can range from mild to extremely hot. The hottest are the green curry pastes.

Curries originated from southern India, but unlike Indian curries, which use a lot of dried powdered spices and are thick and simmered for many hours, Thai curries are fresher and much lighter. They are usually thin and soup-like and require a lot less cooking, with the exception of Mussaman Curry.

Curries in Thailand are always part of a selection of dishes in a main meal and the heat is usually counterbalanced by a blander or sweeter flavoured dish.

Red Chicken Curry with Bamboo Shoots

Bamboo shoots have a lovely crunchy texture. It is quite acceptable to use canned bamboo, as fresh bamboo is not readily available in the West. Whenever you can, buy whole canned bamboo as it is generally crisper and of better quality than sliced shoots. Rinse the bamboo well before using.

INGREDIENTS

Serves 4–6

1 litre/1¾ pint/4 cups coconut milk
450g/1lb diced boneless chicken
30ml/2 tbsp fish sauce
15ml/1 tbsp granulated sugar
225g/8oz bamboo shoots, rinsed
   and sliced
5 kaffir lime leaves, torn
salt and freshly ground black pepper
2 red chillies, chopped, to garnish
10–12 basil leaves, to garnish
10–12 mint leaves, to garnish

For the red curry paste
12–15 red chillies, seeded
4 shallots, thinly sliced
2 garlic cloves, chopped
15ml/1 tbsp chopped galangal
2 stalks lemon grass, chopped
3 kaffir lime leaves, chopped
4 coriander roots
10 black peppercorns
5ml/1 tsp coriander seeds
2.5ml/½ tsp cumin seeds
good pinch of ground cinnamon
5ml/1 tsp ground turmeric
2.5ml/½ tsp shrimp paste
5ml/1 tsp salt
30ml/2 tbsp oil

1 Make the red curry paste. Combine all the ingredients in a mortar, except for the oil, and pound with a pestle, or process in a food processor, until smooth.

2 Add the oil a little at a time and blend in well. Place in a jar in the fridge until ready to use.

3 In a large heavy-based saucepan, bring half the coconut milk to the boil, stirring until it separates.

4 Add 30ml/2 tbsp red curry paste and cook for a few minutes.

5 Add the chicken, fish sauce and sugar. Fry for 3–5 minutes until the chicken changes colour, stirring constantly to prevent it from sticking.

6 Add the rest of the coconut milk, bamboo shoots and kaffir lime leaves. Bring back to the boil. Adjust the seasoning to taste. Serve garnished with chillies, basil and mint leaves.

Bean Curd and Green Bean Red Curry

This is another curry that is simple and quick to make. This recipe uses green beans, but you can use almost any kind of vegetable such as aubergines, bamboo shoots or broccoli.

INGREDIENTS

Serves 4–6

600ml/1 pint/2½ cups coconut milk
15ml/1 tbsp red curry paste
45ml/3 tbsp fish sauce
10ml/2 tsp palm sugar
225g/8oz button mushrooms
115g/4oz green beans, trimmed
175g/6oz bean curd, rinsed and cut
    into 2cm/¾in cubes
4 kaffir lime leaves, torn
2 red chillies, sliced
coriander leaves, to garnish

1 Put about one third of the coconut milk in a wok or saucepan. Cook until it starts to separate and an oily sheen appears.

2 Add the red curry paste, fish sauce and sugar to the coconut milk. Mix together thoroughly.

3 Add the mushrooms. Stir and cook for 1 minute.

4 Stir in the rest of the coconut milk and bring back to the boil.

5 Add the green beans and cubes of bean curd and simmer gently for another 4–5 minutes.

6 Stir in kaffir lime leaves and chillies. Serve garnished with the coriander leaves.

Burmese-style Pork Curry

Burmese-style curries use pork instead of chicken or beef and water rather than coconut milk. The flavours of this delicious dish improve when it is reheated.

INGREDIENTS

Serves 4–6

2.5cm/1in piece fresh root ginger, crushed
8 dried red chillies, soaked in warm water for 20 minutes
2 stalks lemon grass, finely chopped
15ml/1 tbsp chopped galangal
15ml/1 tbsp shrimp paste
30ml/2 tbsp brown sugar
675g/1½lb pork with some of its fat
600ml/1 pint/2½ cups water
10ml/2 tsp ground turmeric
5ml/1 tsp dark soy sauce
4 shallots, finely chopped
15ml/1 tbsp chopped garlic
45ml/3 tbsp tamarind juice
5ml/1 tsp sugar
15ml/1 tbsp fish sauce
green beans, to serve
red chillies, to garnish

1 In a mortar, pound the ginger, chillies, lemon grass and galangal into a coarse paste with a pestle, then add the shrimp paste and brown sugar to produce a dark, grainy purée.

2 Cut the pork into large chunks and place in a large heavy-based saucepan. Add the curry purée and stir to coat the meat thoroughly.

3 Cook over a low heat, stirring occasionally, until the meat has changed colour and rendered some of its fat and the curry paste is fragrant.

4 Stir in the water, turmeric and soy sauce. Simmer gently for about 40 minutes, until the meat is tender.

5 Add the shallots, garlic, tamarind juice, sugar and fish sauce. Serve with freshly cooked green beans, and garnish with chillies.

Thick Beef Curry in Sweet Peanut Sauce

This curry is deliciously rich and thicker than most other Thai curries. Serve with boiled jasmine rice and salted duck's eggs, if liked.

INGREDIENTS

Serves 4–6

600ml/1 pint/2½ cups coconut milk
45ml/3 tbsp red curry paste
45ml/3 tbsp fish sauce
30ml/2 tbsp palm sugar
2 stalks lemon grass, bruised
450g/1lb rump steak cut into
  thin strips
75g/3oz roasted ground peanuts
2 red chillies, sliced
5 kaffir lime leaves, torn
salt and freshly ground black pepper
2 salted eggs, to serve
10–15 Thai basil leaves, to garnish

1 Put half the coconut milk into a heavy-bottomed saucepan and heat, stirring, until it boils and separates.

— COOK'S TIP —

If you don't have the time to make your own red curry paste, you can buy a ready-made Thai curry paste. There is a wide range available in most supermarkets.

2 Add the red curry paste and cook until fragrant. Add the fish sauce, palm sugar and lemon grass.

3 Continue to cook until the colour deepens. Add the rest of the coconut milk. Bring back to the boil.

4 Add the beef and ground peanuts. Stir and cook for 8–10 minutes or until most of the liquid has evaporated.

5 Add the chillies and kaffir lime leaves. Adjust the seasoning to taste. Serve with salted eggs and garnish with Thai basil leaves.

Mussaman Curry

This curry is Indian in origin. Traditionally it is made with beef, but chicken or lamb can be used, or you can make a vegetarian version using bean curd. It has a rich, sweet and spicy flavour.

INGREDIENTS
Serves 4–6
600ml/1 pint/2½ cups coconut milk
675g/1½lb stewing steak, cut into
    2.5cm/1in chunks
250ml/8fl oz/1 cup coconut cream
45ml/3 tbsp Mussaman curry paste
    (see Cook's Tip)
30ml/2 tbsp fish sauce
15ml/1 tbsp palm sugar
60ml/4 tbsp tamarind juice
6 cardamom pods
1 cinnamon stick
225g/8oz potatoes, cut into
    even-size chunks
1 onion, cut into wedges
50g/2oz roasted peanuts
boiled rice, to serve

1 Bring the coconut milk to a gentle boil in a large saucepan. Add the beef and simmer until tender – about 40 minutes.

2 Put the coconut cream into a small saucepan, then cook for about 5–8 minutes, stirring constantly, until it separates.

3 Add the mussaman curry paste and fry until fragrant. Now add the fried curry paste to the pan containing the cooked beef.

— COOK'S TIP —

Musamann curry paste is used to make the Thai version of a Muslim curry. It can be prepared and then stored in a glass jar in the fridge for up to four months.

Remove the seeds from 12 large dried chillies and soak in hot water for 15 minutes. Combine 60ml/4 tbsp chopped shallots, 5 garlic cloves, 1 chopped stalk lemon grass, 10ml/2 tsp chopped galangal, 5 ml/1 tsp cumin seeds, 15ml/1 tbsp coriander seeds, 2 cloves and 6 black peppercorns. Place in a wok and dry-fry over a low heat for 5–6 minutes. Grind or process into a powder and stir in 5ml/1 tsp shrimp paste, 5ml/1 tsp salt, 5ml/1 tsp sugar and 30ml/2tbsp oil.

4 Add the fish sauce, sugar, tamarind juice, cardamom pods, cinnamon stick, potato chunks and onion wedges. Simmer for 10–15 minutes or until the potatoes are cooked.

5 Add the roasted peanuts. Cook for a further 5 minutes. Serve with boiled rice.

Green Beef Curry with Thai Aubergine

This is a very quick curry so be sure to use good quality meat.

INGREDIENTS

Serves 4–6
15ml/1 tbsp vegetable oil
45ml/3 tbsp green curry paste
600ml/1 pint/2½ cups coconut milk
450g/1lb beef sirloin
4 kaffir lime leaves, torn
15–30ml/1–2 tbsp fish sauce
5ml/1 tsp palm sugar
150g/5oz small Thai aubergines, halved
a small handful of Thai basil
2 green chillies, to garnish

For the green curry paste
15 hot green chillies
2 stalks lemon grass, chopped
3 shallots, sliced
2 garlic cloves
15ml/1 tbsp chopped galangal
4 kaffir lime leaves, chopped
2.5ml/½ tsp grated kaffir lime rind
5ml/1 tsp chopped coriander root
6 black peppercorns
5ml/1 tsp coriander seeds, roasted
5ml/1 tsp cumin seeds, roasted
15ml/1 tbsp sugar
5ml/1 tsp salt
5ml/1 tsp shrimp paste (optional)

1 Make the green curry paste. Combine all the ingredients, except for the oil. Pound in a pestle and mortar or process in a food processor until smooth. Add the oil a little at a time and blend well between each addition. Keep in a glass jar in the fridge until required.

2 Heat the oil in a large saucepan or wok. Add 45ml/3 tbsp curry paste and fry until fragrant.

3 Stir in half the coconut milk, a little at a time. Cook for about 5–6 minutes, until an oily sheen appears.

4 Cut the beef into long thin slices and add to the saucepan with the kaffir lime leaves, fish sauce, sugar and aubergines. Cook for 2–3 minutes, then stir in the remaining coconut milk.

5 Bring back to a simmer and cook until the meat and aubergines are tender. Stir in the Thai basil just before serving. Finely shred the green chillies and use to garnish the curry.

Green Curry of Prawns

A popular fragrant creamy curry that also takes very little time to prepare. It can also be made with thin strips of chicken meat.

INGREDIENTS

Serves 4–6
30ml/2 tbsp vegetable oil
30ml/2 tbsp green curry paste
450g/1lb king prawns, shelled
  and deveined
4 kaffir lime leaves, torn
1 stalk lemon grass, bruised
  and chopped
250ml/8fl oz/1 cup coconut milk
30ml/2 tbsp fish sauce
½ cucumber, seeded and cut into thin
  batons
10–15 basil leaves
4 green chillies, sliced, to garnish

1 Heat the oil in a frying pan. Add the green curry paste and fry until bubbling and fragrant.

2 Add the prawns, kaffir lime leaves and lemon grass. Fry for 1–2 minutes, until the prawns are pink.

3 Stir in the coconut milk and bring to a gentle boil. Simmer, stirring occasionally, for about 5 minutes or until the prawns are tender.

4 Stir in the fish sauce, cucumber, and basil, then top with the green chillies and serve.

Pineapple Curry with Prawns and Mussels

The delicate sweet and sour flavour of this curry comes from the pineapple and although it seems an odd combination, it is rather delicious. Use the freshest shellfish that you can find.

INGREDIENTS

Serves 4–6

600ml/1 pint/2½ cups coconut milk
30ml/2 tbsp red curry paste
30ml/2 tbsp fish sauce
15ml/1 tbsp granulated sugar
225g/8oz king prawns, shelled and deveined
450g/1lb mussels, cleaned and beards removed
175g/6oz fresh pineapple, finely crushed or chopped
5 kaffir lime leaves, torn
2 red chillies, chopped, to garnish
coriander leaves, to garnish

1 In a large saucepan, bring half the coconut milk to the boil and heat, stirring, until it separates.

2 Add the red curry paste and cook until fragrant. Add the fish sauce and sugar and continue to cook for a few moments.

3 Stir in the rest of the coconut milk and bring back to the boil. Add the king prawns, mussels, pineapple and kaffir lime leaves.

4 Reheat until boiling and then simmer for 3–5 minutes, until the prawns are cooked and the mussels have opened. Remove any mussels that have not opened and discard. Serve garnished with chopped red chillies and coriander leaves.

Curried Prawns in Coconut Milk

A curry-like dish where the prawns are cooked in a spicy coconut gravy.

INGREDIENTS

Serves 4–6

600ml/1 pint/2½ cups coconut milk
30ml/2 tbsp yellow curry paste (see Cook's Tip)
15ml/1 tbsp fish sauce
2.5ml/½ tsp salt
5ml/1 tsp granulated sugar
450g/1lb king prawns, shelled, tails left intact and deveined
225g/8oz cherry tomatoes
juice of ½ lime, to serve
2 red chillies, cut into strips, to garnish
coriander leaves, to garnish

1 Put half the coconut milk into a pan or wok and bring to the boil.

2 Add the yellow curry paste to the coconut milk, stir until it disperses, then simmer for about 10 minutes.

3 Add the fish sauce, salt, sugar and remaining coconut milk. Simmer for another 5 minutes.

4 Add the prawns and cherry tomatoes. Simmer very gently for about 5 minutes until the prawns are pink and tender.

5 Serve sprinkled with lime juice and garnish with chillies and coriander.

— COOK'S TIP —

To make yellow curry paste, process together 6–8 yellow chillies, 1 chopped lemon grass stalk, 4 peeled shallots, 4 garlic cloves, 15ml/1 tbsp peeled chopped fresh root ginger, 5ml/1 tsp coriander seeds, 5ml/1 tsp mustard powder, 5ml/1 tsp salt, 2.5ml/½ tsp ground cinnamon, 15ml/1 tbsp light brown sugar and 30ml/2 tbsp oil in a blender or food procesor. When a paste has formed, transfer to a glass jar and keep in the fridge.

RICE AND NOODLES

*A bowl of steamy, fluffy rice is essential to any Thai
meal. Rice is a mainstay of Thailand's agriculture
and its principal export. It is therefore treated with
the greatest of respect.*

*There are many varieties of rice, but the most
commonly used are the white, long-grain, fragrant
jasmine rice and the large starchy round-grain also
known as glutinous or sticky rice, which is widely used
in making desserts.*

*After rice, noodles are the second great staple of Asian
kitchens. There are numerous types of noodles and an
even greater number of noodle dishes. They make a
nutritious and satisfying one-dish meal and are popular
for lunch, breakfast or as a snack.*

Coconut Rice

This rich dish is usually served with a tangy papaya salad.

INGREDIENTS

Serves 4–6

450g/1lb/2 cups jasmine rice
250ml/8fl oz/1 cup water
475ml/16fl oz/2 cups coconut milk
2.5ml/½ tsp salt
30ml/2 tbsp granulated sugar
fresh shredded coconut, to garnish
   (optional)

1 Wash the rice in several changes of cold water until it runs clear. Place the water, coconut milk, salt and sugar in a heavy-bottomed saucepan.

2 Add the rice, cover and bring to the boil. Reduce the heat to low and simmer for about 15–20 minutes or until the rice is tender to the bite and cooked through.

3 Turn off the heat and allow the rice to rest in the saucepan for a further 5–10 minutes.

4 Fluff up the rice with chopsticks before serving.

Pineapple Fried Rice

When buying a pineapple, look for a sweet-smelling fruit with an even brownish/yellow skin. To test for ripeness, tap the base – a dull sound indicates that the fruit is ripe. The flesh should also give slightly when pressed.

INGREDIENTS

Serves 4–6

1 pineapple
30ml/2 tbsp vegetable oil
1 small onion, finely chopped
2 green chillies, seeded and chopped
225g/8oz lean pork, cut into
   small dice
115g/4oz cooked shelled prawns
675–900g/1½–2 lb/3–4 cups cooked
   cold rice
50g/2oz roasted cashew nuts
2 spring onions, chopped
30ml/2 tbsp fish sauce
15ml/1 tbsp soy sauce
10–12 mint leaves, to garnish
2 red chillies, sliced, to garnish
1 green chilli, sliced, to garnish

1 Cut the pineapple in half lengthways and remove the flesh from both halves by cutting round inside the skin. Reserve the skin shells. You need 115g/4oz of fruit, chopped finely (keep the rest for a dessert).

--- COOK'S TIP ---

This dish is ideal to prepare for a special occasion meal. Served in the pineapple skin shells, it is sure to be the talking point of the dinner.

2 Heat the oil in a wok or large frying pan. Add the onion and chillies and fry for about 3–5 minutes until softened. Add the pork and cook until it is brown on all sides.

3 Stir in the prawns and rice and toss well together. Continue to stir-fry until the rice is thoroughly heated.

4 Add the chopped pineapple, cashew nuts and spring onions. Season with fish sauce and soy sauce.

5 Spoon into the pineapple skin shells. Garnish with shredded mint leaves and red and green chillies.

Jasmine Rice

A naturally aromatic, long grain white rice, jasmine rice is the staple of most Thai meals. If you eat rice regularly, you might want to invest in an electric rice cooker.

INGREDIENTS

Serves 4–6

450g/1lb/2 cups jasmine rice
750ml/1¼ pint/3 cups cold water

------ COOK'S TIP ------

An electric rice cooker cooks the rice and keeps it warm. Different sizes and models of rice cookers are available. The top of the range is a non-stick version, which is expensive, but well worth the money

1 Rinse the rice thoroughly at least three times in cold water until the water runs clear.

2 Put the rice in a heavy-based saucepan and add the water. Bring the rice to a vigorous boil, uncovered, over a high heat.

3 Stir and reduce the heat to low. Cover and simmer for up to 20 minutes, or until all the water has been absorbed. Remove from the heat and leave to stand for 10 minutes.

4 Remove the lid and stir the rice gently with a rice paddle or a pair of wooden chopsticks, to fluff up and separate the grains.

Fried Jasmine Rice with Prawns and Thai Basil

Thai basil (*bai grapao*), also known as Holy basil, has a unique, pungent flavour that is both spicy and sharp. It can be found in most Oriental food markets.

INGREDIENTS

Serves 4–6

45ml/3 tbsp vegetable oil
1 egg, beaten
1 onion, chopped
15ml/1 tbsp chopped garlic
15ml/1 tbsp shrimp paste
1kg/2¼lb/4 cups cooked jasmine rice
350g/12oz cooked shelled prawns
50g/2oz thawed frozen peas
oyster sauce, to taste
2 spring onions, chopped
15–20 Thai basil leaves, roughly snipped, plus an extra sprig, to garnish

1 Heat 15ml/1 tbsp of the oil in a wok or frying pan. Add the beaten egg and swirl it around the pan to set like a thin pancake.

2 Cook until golden, slide out on to a board, roll up and cut into thin strips. Set aside.

3 Heat the remaining oil in the wok, add the onion and garlic and fry for 2–3 minutes. Stir in the shrimp paste and mix well.

4 Add the rice prawns and peas and toss and stir together, until everything is heated through.

5 Season with oyster sauce to taste, taking great care as the shrimp paste is salty. Add the spring onions and basil leaves. Transfer to a serving dish and serve topped with the strips of egg pancake. Garnish with a sprig of basil.

Fried Rice with Pork

If liked, garnish with strips of egg omelette, as in the Jasmine Rice with Prawns and Holy Basil.

INGREDIENTS

Serves 4–6

45ml/3 tbsp vegetable oil
1 onion, chopped
15ml/1 tbsp chopped garlic
115g/4oz pork, cut into small cubes
2 eggs, beaten
1kg/2¼lb/4 cups cooked rice
30ml/2 tbsp fish sauce
15ml/1 tbsp dark soy sauce
2.5 ml/½ tsp caster sugar
4 spring onions, finely sliced, to garnish
2 red chillies, sliced, to garnish
1 lime, cut into wedges, to garnish
egg omelette, to garnish (optional)

1 Heat the oil in a wok or large frying pan. Add the onion and garlic and cook for about 2 minutes until softened.

2 Add the pork to the softened onion and garlic. Stir-fry until the pork changes colour and is cooked.

3 Add the eggs and cook until scrambled into small lumps.

4 Add the rice and continue to stir and toss, to coat it with the oil and prevent it from sticking.

5 Add the fish sauce, soy sauce and sugar and mix well. Continue to fry until the rice is thoroughly heated. Garnish with sliced spring onion, red chillies and lime wedges. Top with a few strips of egg omelette, if you like.

Special Chow Mein

Lap cheong is a special air-dried Chinese sausage. It is available from most Chinese supermarkets. If you cannot buy it, substitute with either diced ham, chorizo or salami.

INGREDIENTS

Serves 4–6

45ml/3 tbsp vegetable oil
2 garlic cloves, sliced
5ml/1 tsp chopped fresh root ginger
2 red chillies, chopped
2 lap cheong, about 75g/3oz, rinsed
  and sliced (optional)
1 boneless chicken breast, thinly sliced
16 uncooked tiger prawns, peeled, tails
  left intact, and deveined
115g/4oz green beans
225g/8oz beansprouts
50g/2oz garlic chives
450g/1lb egg noodles, cooked in
  boiling water until tender
30ml/2 tbsp soy sauce
15ml/1 tbsp oyster sauce
salt and freshly ground black pepper
15ml/1 tbsp sesame oil
2 spring onions, shredded, to garnish
15ml/1 tbsp coriander leaves,
  to garnish

1 Heat 15ml/1 tbsp of the oil in a wok or large frying pan and fry the garlic, ginger and chillies. Add the lap cheong, chicken, prawns and beans. Stir-fry for about 2 minutes over a high heat or until the chicken and prawns are cooked. Transfer the mixture to a bowl and set aside.

2 Heat the rest of the oil in the same wok. Add the beansprouts and garlic chives. Stir fry for 1–2 minutes.

3 Add the noodles and toss and stir to mix. Season with soy sauce, oyster sauce, salt and pepper.

4 Return the prawn mixture to the wok. Reheat and mix well with the noodles. Stir in the sesame oil. Serve garnished with spring onions and coriander leaves.

Crispy Fried Rice Vermicelli

Mee Krob is usually served at celebration meals. It is a crisp tangle of fried rice vermicelli, which is tossed in a piquant garlic, sweet and sour sauce.

INGREDIENTS

Serves 4–6
oil for frying
175g/6oz rice vermicelli
15ml/1 tbsp chopped garlic
4–6 dried chillies, seeded and chopped
30ml/2 tbsp chopped shallot
15ml/1 tbsp dried shrimps, rinsed
115g/4oz minced pork
115g/4oz uncooked shelled prawns, chopped
30ml/2 tbsp brown bean sauce
30ml/2 tbsp rice wine vinegar
45ml/3 tbsp fish sauce
75g/3 tbsp palm sugar
30ml/2 tbsp tamarind or lime juice
115g/4oz beansprouts

For the garnish
2 spring onions, shredded
30ml/2 tbsp fresh coriander leaves
2 heads pickled garlic (optional)
2-egg omelette, rolled and sliced
2 red chillies, chopped

1 Heat the oil in a wok. Break the rice vermicelli apart into small handfuls about 7.5cm/3in long. Deep fry in the hot oil until they puff up. Remove and drain on kitchen paper.

2 Leave 30ml/2 tbsp of the hot oil in the wok, add the garlic, chillies, shallots and shrimps. Fry until fragrant.

3 Add the minced pork and stir-fry for about 3–4 minutes, until it is no longer pink. Add the prawns and fry for a further 2 minutes. Remove the mixture and set aside.

4 To the same wok, add the brown bean sauce, vinegar, fish sauce and palm sugar. Bring to a gentle boil, stir to dissolve the sugar and cook until thick and syrupy.

5 Add the tamarind or lime juice and adjust the seasoning. It should be sweet, sour and salty.

6 Reduce the heat. Add the pork and prawn mixture and the beansprouts to the sauce; stir to mix.

7 Add the rice noodles and toss gently to coat them with the sauce without breaking the noodles too much. Transfer the noodles to a platter. Garnish with spring onions, coriander leaves, pickled garlic, omelette strips and red chillies.

Thai Fried Noodles

Phat Thai has a fascinating flavour and texture. It is made with rice noodles and is considered one of the national dishes of Thailand.

INGREDIENTS

Serves 4–6
350g/12oz rice noodles
45ml/3 tbsp vegetable oil
15ml/1 tbsp chopped garlic
16 uncooked king prawns, shelled, tails
  left intact and deveined
2 eggs, lightly beaten
15ml/1 tbsp dried shrimps, rinsed
30ml/2 tbsp pickled white radish
50g/2oz fried bean curd, cut into
  small slivers
2.5ml/½ tsp dried chilli flakes
115g/4oz garlic chives, cut into
  5cm/2in lengths
225g/8oz beansprouts
50g/2oz roasted peanuts, coarsely
  ground
5ml/1 tsp granulated sugar
15ml/1 tbsp dark soy sauce
30ml/2 tbsp fish sauce
30ml/2 tbsp tamarind juice
30ml/2 tbsp coriander leaves,
  to garnish
1 kaffir lime, to garnish

1 Soak the noodles in warm water for 20–30 minutes, then drain.

2 Heat 15ml/1 tbsp of the oil in a wok or large frying pan. Add the garlic and fry until golden. Stir in the prawns and cook for about 1–2 minutes until pink, tossing from time to time. Remove and set aside.

3 Heat another 15ml/1 tbsp of oil in the wok. Add the eggs and tilt the wok to spread them into a thin sheet. Stir to scramble and break the egg into small pieces. Remove from the wok and set aside with the prawns.

4 Heat the remaining oil in the same wok. Add the dried shrimps, pickled radish, bean curd and dried chillies. Stir briefly. Add the soaked noodles and stir-fry for 5 minutes.

5 Add the garlic chives, half the beansprouts and half the peanuts. Season with the granulated sugar, soy sauce, fish sauce and tamarind juice. Mix well and cook until the noodles are heated through.

6 Return the prawn and egg mixture to the wok and mix with the noodles. Serve garnished with the rest of the beansprouts, peanuts, coriander leaves and lime wedges.

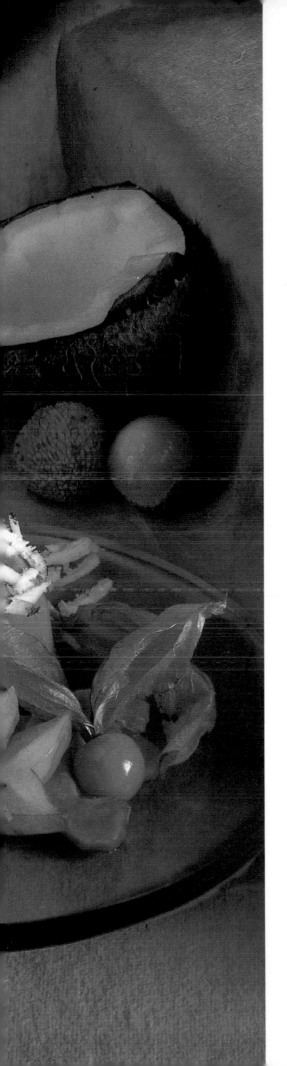

DESSERTS

Thais, unlike many of their Asian neighbours, take great pride in their desserts and consider it an essential and harmonious way of rounding off a balanced meal. Most are based on Thailand's wonderful fruits. The simplest is a platter of fresh tropical fruits, often carved into appealing shapes. Depending on the season, these fruits may include pawpaw, mangoes, custard apple, mangosteen, ramhutans, durian and jackfruits. Other fruits, such as banana and pineapple, can be fried in batter to make delicious fritters.

Very often, desserts are eaten in between meals to serve as a snack, which explains why some Thai desserts are quite rich and filling.

Coconut milk, an essential ingredient of both savoury and sweet dishes, is often incorporated into the dessert menu in one form or another, as in pumpkin stewed with coconut milk and baked coconut custard.

Tapioca Pudding

This pudding, made from large pearl tapioca and coconut milk and served warm, is much lighter than the western-style version. You can adjust the sweetness to your taste. Serve with lychees or the smaller, similar-tasting logans – also known as 'dragon's eyes'.

INGREDIENTS

Serves 4
115g/4oz tapioca
475ml/16fl oz/2 cups water
175g/6oz granulated sugar
pinch of salt
250ml/8fl oz/1 cup coconut milk
250g/9oz prepared tropical fruits
finely shredded rind of 1 lime,
　to decorate

1 Soak the tapioca in warm water for 1 hour so the grains swell. Drain.

2 Put the water in a saucepan and bring to the boil. Stir in the sugar and salt.

3 Add the tapioca and coconut milk and simmer for 10 minutes or until the tapioca turns transparent.

4 Serve warm with some tropical fruits and decorate with lime zest strips and coconut shavings, if using.

Fried Bananas

These delicious treats are a favourite among children and adults alike. They are sold as snacks throughout the day and night at portable roadside stalls and market places. Other fruits such as pineapple and apple work just as well.

INGREDIENTS

Serves 4
115g/4oz plain flour
2.5ml/½ tsp bicarbonate of soda
pinch of salt
30ml/2 tbsp granulated sugar
1 egg
90ml/6 tbsp water
30ml/2 tbsp shredded coconut or
　15ml/1 tbsp sesame seeds
4 firm bananas
oil for frying
30ml/2 tbsp honey, to serve (optional)
sprigs of mint, to decorate

1 Sift the flour, bicarbonate of soda and salt into a bowl. Stir in the granulated sugar. Whisk in the egg and add enough water to make quite a thin batter.

2 Whisk in the shredded coconut or sesame seeds.

3 Peel the bananas. Carefully cut each one in half lengthways, then in half crossways.

4 Heat the oil in a wok or deep frying pan. Dip the bananas in the batter, then gently drop a few into the oil. Fry until golden brown.

5 Remove from the oil and drain on kitchen paper. Serve immediately with honey, if using, and decorate with sprigs of mint.

Baked Rice Pudding, Thai-style

Black glutinous rice, also known as black sticky rice, has long black grains and a nutty taste similar to wild rice. This baked pudding has a distinct character and flavour all of its own.

Ingredients

Serves 4–6
175g/6oz white or black glutinous (sticky) rice
30ml/2 tbsp soft light brown sugar
475ml/16fl oz/2 cups coconut milk
250ml/8fl oz/1 cup water
3 eggs
30ml/2 tbsp granulated sugar

1 Combine the glutinous rice, brown sugar, half the coconut milk and all the water in a saucepan.

2 Bring to the boil and simmer for about 15–20 minutes or until the rice has absorbed most of the liquid, stirring from time to time. Preheat the oven to 150°C/300°F/Gas 3.

3 Transfer the rice into one large ovenproof dish or divide it between individual ramekins. Mix together the eggs, remaining coconut milk and sugar in a bowl.

4 Strain and pour the mixture evenly over the par-cooked rice.

5 Place the dish in a baking tin. Pour in enough boiling water to come halfway up the sides of the dish.

6 Cover the dish with a piece of foil and bake in the oven for about 35 minutes to 1 hour or until the custard is set. Serve warm or cold.

Mango with Sticky Rice

Everyone's favourite dessert. Mangoes, with their delicate fragrance, sweet and sour flavour and velvety flesh, blend especially well with coconut sticky rice. You need to start preparing this dish the day before.

Ingredients

Serves 4
115g/4oz sticky (glutinous) white rice
175ml/6fl oz/¾ cup thick coconut milk
45ml/3 tbsp granulated sugar
pinch of salt
2 ripe mangoes
strips of lime rind, to decorate

1 Rinse the glutinous rice thoroughly in several changes of cold water, then leave to soak overnight in a bowl of fresh, cold water.

2 Drain and spread the rice in an even layer in a steamer lined with cheesecloth. Cover and steam for about 20 minutes or until the grains of rice are tender.

3 Meanwhile, reserve 45ml/3 tbsp of the top of the coconut milk and combine the rest with the sugar and salt in a saucepan. Bring to the boil, stirring until the sugar dissolves, then pour into a bowl and leave to cool a little.

4 Turn the rice into a bowl and pour over the coconut mixture. Stir, then leave for about 10–15 minutes.

5 Peel the mangoes and cut the flesh into slices. Place on top of the rice and drizzle over the reserved coconut milk. Decorate with strips of lime rind.

Coconut Custard

This traditional dish can be baked or steamed and is often served with sweet sticky rice and a selection of fruit such as mango and tamarillo.

INGREDIENTS

Serves 4–6
4 eggs
75g/3oz soft light brown sugar
250ml/8fl oz/1 cup coconut milk
5ml/1 tsp vanilla, rose or
  jasmine extract
mint leaves, to decorate
icing sugar, to decorate

1 Preheat the oven to 150°C/300°F/ Gas 2. Whisk the eggs and sugar in a bowl until smooth. Add the coconut milk and vanilla or other extract and blend well together.

2 Strain the mixture and pour into individual ramekins or a cake tin.

3 Stand the ramekins or tin in a roasting pan. Carefully fill the pan with hot water to reach halfway up the outsides of the ramekins or tin.

4 Bake for about 35–40 minutes or until the custards are set. Test with a fine skewer or cocktail stick.

5 Remove from the oven and leave to cool. Turn out onto a plate, and serve with sliced fruit. Decorate with mint leaves and icing sugar.

Stewed Pumpkin in Coconut Cream

Stewed fruit is a popular dessert in Thailand. Use the firm-textured Japanese kabocha pumpkin for this dish, if you can. Bananas and melons can also be prepared in this way and you can even stew sweetcorn kernels or pulses such as mung beans and black beans in coconut milk.

INGREDIENTS

Serves 4–6

1kg/2¼lb kabocha pumpkin
750ml/1¼ pint/3 cups coconut milk
175g/6oz granulated sugar
pinch of salt
pumpkin seed kernels, toasted, and
  mint sprigs, to decorate

1 Wash the pumpkin skin and cut off most of it. Scoop out the seeds.

COOK'S TIP

Any pumpkin can be used for this dish, as long as it has a firm texture. Jamaican or New Zealand varieties both make good alternatives to kabocha pumpkin.

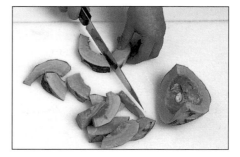

2 Using a sharp knife, cut the flesh into pieces about 5cm/2in long and 2cm/¾in thick.

3 In a saucepan, bring the coconut milk, sugar and salt to the boil.

4 Add the pumpkin and simmer for about 10–15 minutes until the pumpkin is tender. Serve warm. Decorate each serving with a mint sprig and a few toasted pumpkin seed kernels.

Index